"Players and coaches of all ages can gain great insight into the art of hitting by reading and digesting Bernardo Leonard's *The Superstar Hitter's Bible*. I found the combining of both the physical and mental elements of hitting throughout the book to be superb. I rely on one man to keep my team hitting: Bernardo Leonard."

—Coach Jim Ellwanger
Incarnate Word College
San Antonio, Texas

"I have never read a book about hitting with the depth and understanding that Bernardo Leonard brings to it. *The Superstar Hitter's Bible* should be at the bedside of anyone who seeks to hit a baseball, whether he's a Little Leaguer or a big leaguer."

—Vince Coleman

"There is one superstar on the horizon today with the knowledge and understanding to teach an amateur and help any pro to hit a baseball, and that man is Bernardo Leonard. His *Superstar Hitter's Bible* is a masterpiece."

—Hubie Brooks

"Bernardo has a great knowledge of the hitting game. Listen to what the man has to say."

—Matt Williams

THE Superstar HITTER'S BIBLE

THE Superstar HITTER'S BIBLE

Winning Tips, Techniques, and Strategies from Baseball's Top Players

Bernardo Leonard, Zen Master and Hitting Guru, and Peter Golenbock

CB
CONTEMPORARY BOOKS

Library of Congress Cataloging-in-Publication Data

Leonard, Bernardo.
    The superstar hitter's bible : featuring the 20 commandments of
hitting / by Bernardo Leonard and Peter Golenbock ; with commentary
by Cecil Fielder . . . [et al.].
        p.   cm.
    ISBN 0-8092-3000-3
    1. Batting (Baseball)   I. Golenbock, Peter, 1946–   .   II. Title.
GV869.L46   1998
796.357'26—dc21   97-40103
                                                CIP

Cover design by Todd Petersen
Cover photograph copyright © 1997 David Madison
Interior design by Nick Panos
Interior illustrations by Dan Krovatin

Published by Contemporary Books
An imprint of NTC/Contemporary Publishing Group, Inc.
4255 West Touhy Avenue, Lincolnwood (Chicago), Illinois 60646-1975 U.S.A.
Printed in the United States of America
International Standard Book Number: 0-8092-3000-3
18   17   16   15   14   13   12   11   10   9   8   7   6   5   4   3   2   1

Contents

Foreword

by Peter Golenbock

Sometimes a person will come into your life with the rush of a hurricane. Bernardo Leonard was like that. We met in the winter of 1989 during the first and only complete season of the late, lamented Senior League, a six-team league for former major league baseball players over the age of thirty-five. At the end of the season Bernardo called to say he wanted to write a book about hitting. I put him off.

Bernardo had reached Class AAA in the Detroit Tiger organization, but he had no name recognition. He was one of the better players for a woefully overage St. Lucie Legends team. I was impressed with his playing ability. But I could not imagine that he could tell me any more about hitting than I already knew, which was a considerable amount. I had written a hitting book with Pete Rose, arguably the best hitter in the history of the game. And I had coached baseball from high school to Little League for more than thirty years, and usually my players hit just fine.

But Bernardo was persistent, wouldn't take *no* for an answer, demanded I let him come over. And once Bernardo got me to sit still long enough to listen, quickly it became clear to me that when it comes to hitting, Bernardo Leonard is Michelangelo, Leonardo DaVinci, or Picasso. He is a sheer genius on the subject, and everyone else who considers himself knowledgable in the art of hitting a baseball is just a rube in comparison. I suspect you are as cynical as I was. You'll see. I was wrong when I thought I knew everything there was to know about hitting, and you will find you are, too.

As you will soon see, I am not exaggerating about Bernardo. We have called this book *The Superstar Hitter's Bible* because it is an accurate title. If there is the slightest flaw in your swing, you will be able to discover what it is and correct it. Turns out, Bernardo Leonard is the man the top pros go to for advice. For many years behind the scenes, Bernardo Leonard has tutored some of baseball's greatest players, many of whom you will hear from in this book. He has managed to break down the seemingly simple movement of swinging a bat at a ball into its minutest parts. He will explain the proper mechanics of each small part of the swing and tell you exactly how it affects your ability to hit the ball.

One word of caution: this is not a book to be read quickly or in one sitting. Almost every sentence in this book has importance. If you are sincere about wanting to improve your hitting, you will have to study this book as you would any textbook. Read each piece of advice slowly and carefully, and with your bat in hand, try to do exactly what Bernardo tells you. Then go back and reread it again and again.

Go through the book, page by page, studying the mechanics of hitting in chapters one through six. The rest of the book is concerned with the mental part of hitting, which is just as important as the physical part. It may be that you can't hit well because you are taking the wrong mental approach. Make sure you closely read the second half of the book.

If you are impatient, have trouble sitting down and reading a book, or want the quick fix, my advice is first to concentrate on the twenty commandments, the most important pillars of advice on hitting. Perhaps after studying the commandments, you will find Bernardo's instructions so useful and interesting you will make time to read the tips as well.

If you are one of those people who believe hitting is done by instinct alone and no amount of teaching will make you a better hitter, I advise you, for once in your life, to put away the ignorance-is-bliss approach and give Bernardo's lessons a try. You will be amazed how much improvement you will see. Ignorance may be bliss, but knowledge is power, both in life and at the plate.

Introduction

The Art of Hitting: What a Feeling!

This book is called a bible because it will guide you to your promised land—becoming a productive, powerful batter. And I can say this because for years I've watched these methods work their magic on such teams as the Little League champions of Taiwan; professional teams from Cuba, Mexico, Italy, the Netherlands, and Australia; and on some of the great players in the game, such as Ryne Sandberg, Tim Raines, Tony Gwynn, Hubie Brooks, Mark Grace, Ozzie Smith, Kevin Bass, and Willie McGee.

In every single hitting book that has ever been written, the author's first sentence sounds something like this: "The most difficult job in any sport is hitting a baseball." It has almost become a cliché. Of course, there is good reason this sentiment appears so often. Hitting surely IS the single most difficult task in all of sports. Ty Cobb had the highest batting average in the history of the game, yet for every hundred at bats, he still made an out sixty-four times.

Bernardo Leonard instructing in Taiwan

Teaching batting techniques to two hundred Taiwanese baseball coaches

The reason hitting a baseball safely is so difficult is that the task involves many factors, some of which are out of your control. On the major league level, the speed, variety of pitches, and control of the pitchers keep improving, and so does the skill of the fielders. Imagine how hard it must have been to face Todd Worrell's 90 MPH fastball with Ozzie Smith, Tommy Herr, and Terry Pendleton standing behind him ready to field the ball.

It takes the average major league fastball four-tenths of a second to travel the distance to the plate. The hitter must see the pitch; judge the velocity, rotation, location, and trajectory; and complete a solid, smooth swing faster than it takes to say "Nolan Ryan." That's a lot to do in a very short period of time.

Hitting is so difficult that even the most studious hitters try to keep it simple. I've spent hours and hours working on and thinking about this art to try to reduce it to its simplest terms. This book will teach you the correct mechanics and give you the mental edge to become a serious threat at the plate by providing a series of tips and techniques I call the twenty commandments of hitting. I need twice as many as Moses did. That's how difficult hitting is.

This is a book about hitting. It is also a book about learning. In studying my teaching methods and theories, it is important that you re-examine the way you approach your hitting game. This book is not simply a compilation of tips and techniques, though you will discover plenty of new and revolutionary aids and ideas here. You must read along as a dazzling array of hitting stars and I break hitting into its components. You must internalize the different steps along the way, become comfortable with everything you learn, and finally, after hours of practice, discover the hitting genius within you.

Let me ask you this very important question: which is more important in hitting a baseball, the physical technique or the mental approach?

The answer: both are equally important.

To be a successful hitter, you must master the physical and the mental. The mind can stop you from succeeding just as the body can. You can have excellent mechanics and still not hit well. At the same time, you can know intellectually what pitch to look for, but if you don't have the correct mechanics, even if you get the pitch you're looking for, you will not be able to hit it. The secret is to select a series of helpful techniques regarding swinging the bat and *thinking* about swinging the bat that will result in peak performance.

As for the physical part of hitting, I am convinced that because there are so many components to the swing, a perfect swing is rare. It is virtually impossible to swing at a pitch without doing something wrong. The goal, then, is to do as many of these components as perfectly as possible, and hope the end result is a hard-hit ball that eludes the grasp of a fielder (or goes over his head and out of the ballpark).

After years of working with many of the best major league hitters in the game, I have learned that *everyone* has batting flaws and those flaws usually come from bad habits learned during childhood. The primary reason youngsters learn so many bad habits is they are usually first taught by amateurs—coaches or parents who don't know the proper techniques of hitting.

Another major reason for bad batting habits is that youngsters like to imitate childhood heroes. This can be disastrous, but I see it all the time. Just because Jeff Bagwell or Ken Griffey Jr. or Barry Bonds hits a certain way doesn't mean that will be the right way for you. In fact, it probably will be the *wrong* way for you. Bad habits, I've discovered, are very easy to form.

Once we adopt a style, even if the technique is wrong, we imprint that style by performing the actions time and time again until we do them without thinking on a conscious level. They become so much a part of us that we take them for granted. We find it difficult to even imagine doing what we do habitually in any other way. There's a reason for this. If every time you wanted to swing a bat you had to do it consciously, you would never get the bat off your shoulders.

Because habits are a product of the mind, we must effectively find a way to deal with the fact that the only way to improve at bat is to change bad habits. It's not as easy to do as you might think.

You must recognize that even though you hit in a certain way, that way may not be the best way. You must recognize that there may be a fear within you against making changes in the way you hit. The wise person will accept the notion that improvement will come only after he becomes open to new ideas and adopts new techniques that produce better results.

An important goal of this book is to get you to unlearn bad habits and to reorient your thinking by teaching you the proper habits. There is only one correct way for each individual hitter to be successful, and finding that right way is possible with an open mind and a trial-and-error system of experimenting with workable combinations.

After you read the twenty commandments of hitting, you will understand what constitutes the perfect grip, stance, stride, swing, and follow through. You will also know just what to look for and how to respond, and I guarantee you will be a better hitter because you will be taking a higher percentage of good swings at good pitches.

This book will help any hitter find that perfect combination of movements that will result in a higher batting average and greater consistency and power. No matter how good you are, whether you're a Little Leaguer or a major leaguer, you'll discover a way to improve.

How much you improve will depend on how well you control your mind. There are two types of hitters, even on the major league level. There are hitters who swing the bat, and there are hitters who swing the bat with knowledge of what they are doing. This is the mental part of the art and skill of hitting. Some players go through their entire careers without achieving success. Often the reason is they played their entire careers without the mental road map to lead them down the proper path. And it's a shame. But hitting is such a mystical skill, there are very few knowledegeable instructors to guide you. Without trying to sound like I am boasting, I will say that if you follow the instructions in this book and practice what you are told, you will find what you've been missing. Once you follow the commandments of hitting and understand the principles, you will discover the beauty of going up to the plate with confidence and inner strength.

The mind holds the key to thought, memory, emotion, and creativity, the very qualities that make us human. All these things are involved in hitting. Hitting a baseball is an everyday activity we can do without thinking about it, yet this simple action involves a complex sequence of observation, decision, and movement or coordinated activity inside the body.

When you step into the batter's box, instinct takes over. Once you're there, you don't have time to think. Thinking is an inner function. Hitting is an outer function.

As the ball comes in flight, your eyes follow its path. Messages race along the nerves connecting your eyes to your brain. The information is evaluated to tell you the ball's speed, path, and how quickly it should reach you. Meanwhile, messages are spreading along other nerves to signal muscles to move your head and eyes to keep the ball in sight. You begin to move your hands into a position where you can hit the ball in flight and balance your body so as not to fall in the process of swinging.

At the back of the brain is a structure called the cerebellum, which coordinates body movements. As you practice a physical action, you get better at it. This is what I call skill memory. Hitting is concerned with less conscious learning, which is acquired by repeated actions. In other words, once you have read and understood the proper techniques of the skill of hitting, practice, practice, and more practice is the only way to achieve permanent improvement. Reading this book without going into the batting cage and using what you learn will significantly slow your ability to improve.

A player must be committed to work because he will only get back what he puts in. George Brett, the great Kansas City Royals hitting star, once said, "Every time you are not practicing, someone else is, and if you ever meet him, he'll win."

Hitting well results from going out and playing. These featured major leaguers and I will give you information to use in order to find the optimal comfort level and the right feel.

As a hitter, you must learn patience. As a student of hitting, you must *be* patient. Improvement does not come immediately, but over time with practice. Bad habits are hard to break. If you have learned something wrong, you will find it extremely hard to unlearn. But if you study the proper techniques and are patient, success will be yours. I guarantee it—if you have the will-power to make it happen.

Controlling your mind is important for another reason. It will be impossible to become a successful hitter if you go up to the plate with fear. One obvious fear, of course, is the fear of the ball. I have to assume that you as a batter have mastered that fear. No one can teach a hitter not to be afraid of the ball. Only experience and time can erase such a fear.

But there is another kind of fear that must be mastered—the fear of change.

Every batter has his own style of hitting, and a batter, even one in the major leagues, can become very protective of his personal style. It may be a style he's used for years, and even if it's not particularly successful, that batter will continue to use that style because he may be afraid to change. Fear motivates a batter to resist change and refuse to accept coaching and advice. If you are stubborn and refuse to change and make adjustments in order to improve, I am afraid you are doomed to mediocrity.

Failure is the result of not being able to achieve an objective. In hitting, the greater your knowledge, the less failure you create for yourself, and the more confidence you gain. Confidence inspires improvement and personal growth. This book will provide knowledge.

When you have internalized everything in this book, knowledge of the proper physical and mental techniques will give you unhesitating and effortless movement, absent any conflicting notion in the mind, giving you absolute confidence to be the hitter you've always wanted to be. It will give you a sense of place and comfort and a state of mind that will give you the mental advantage over any pitcher.

In the process of doing that, you will change your mental attitude from one of fear, tension, and indecision to one of confidence that will enable you to be aggressive in welcoming the challenge without fear of failure.

When you have mastered both the physical and mental aspects of the game, I promise you will feel more comfortable at the plate and, most important, more confident, until one day you will discover that when you step up to hit, a calm will settle over you. You will not worry about your mechanics. You won't care who is pitching. You will know in your heart that you are going to be successful.

Your concentration will be so focused that in every at bat you will see nothing but the pitcher's arm, his release, and the ball. Even at high speeds that ball will look as big as a grapefruit, and when it approaches the plate you won't be fooled—the ball will be right where you expected it. And when you hit it, the swing will be effortless. You will hit it hard and it will go a long way.

This feeling is the hitter's nirvana. There is no way to will it to come. It comes from within. All I can tell you is that when it comes, you will know it is there, and you will hope that feeling stays with you for a long time.

Pitching is glamorous, but hitting is exciting. Taking a perfect swing and hitting a line drive feels so very special. Study. Learn. Practice.

Then feel the magic.

THE Superstar HITTER'S BIBLE

PART I

Mastering the Physical Aspects of Hitting

CHAPTER 1

THE RIGHT BAT

There is nothing more personal to a hitter than the size of his bat. These days batters are using bats of all shapes, sizes, and colors. There are wide grains, tight grains, thin handles, thick handles, big barrels, small barrels, and bats that are cupped at the end. Not to mention aluminum bats.

Which should you choose? There is only one criteria: you *must* choose a bat that is comfortable and well-balanced.

The balance of a bat comes from the proportion of the weight to the length. When you find the correct balance, the result will be a quick, controlled swing. There is no formula for selecting the right bat. The bat must *feel* right. It must be light enough, and you must feel quick enough to use it.

TIP: Select a bat as long and heavy as you can control.

There is a balancing point—a trade-off—to be made between the weight of the bat (which gives it momentum) and the length of the bat (which controls the elapsed time of the swing). A bat that is too heavy will result in a slow swing, loss of balance during the swing, loss of optical vision, and a bad path as you swing at the ball. If the bat is too light you may not be able to feel the bat head. If you can't feel where the bat head is, you will suffer a loss of control. In addition, when you swing your lead shoulder will always open up too soon.

It takes less time to swing a short bat than a long one, but shorter bats provide less power than longer ones. If you pick a bat that is too short, you give away power you should be using. If you pick one that's too long, the result will be loss of control. The better balanced your bat, the more control you'll have at the plate. The selection of the bat is a mental process because it's done by feel. Your confidence as a hitter is directly related to the feel and balance of the bat in your hands.

Choose your bat based on your physical strength and your hand size. The stronger you are, the bigger and longer the bat you can handle. Never use a bat that feels too heavy or is weighted too much at the end.

Picking the Right Bat

The coach (parent) grips the bat at the barrel end and extends it toward the hitter. The hitter places the bat across the palm of his bottom hand with the palm facing upward and then wraps fingers and thumb around the grip in a comfortable position. The coach (parent) then releases the bat.

If the hitter cannot control the barrel end of the bat—if it drops more than an inch or two—it is too heavy, too long, or both. The grip of the bottom hand should be firm, with most of the grip strength coming from the middle two fingers.

TIPS: If you have large hands, you will be able to swing any bat, thin-handled or thick. If you have small hands, it is wise to stick to a bat with a thin handle.

If you are a hitter with slow hands, choose a bat with a thick handle. You will get jammed often and with a thick-handled bat those balls might go over the infield rather than splinter the bat. If you are a long-ball hitter or a batter with quick hands, opt for a thin-handled bat because you can generate better bat speed. For the contact or spray hitter, choose a thick-handled bat.

If you choose a thin-handled bat, decrease the weight of the bat so it does not feel top-heavy. With a thick-handled bat, increase the weight so it will not feel out of balance.

One option for major leaguers who use wooden bats is the cupped bat. Cupped bats are heavier than other bats. But the cup at the top of the bat reduces the weight at the head and the result is a combination of solid wood and increased bat speed.

Because hitting is such an individual skill, some hitters break all guidelines when choosing a bat. Note that former Kansas City Royals first baseman Willie Aikens, a strong man with large hands who weighs about 240 pounds, preferred a light, short bat. Jack Clark, one of the great power hitters in the game, used a short, light bat.

Whatever bat you choose, you will find there will be days when it doesn't feel comfortable. The reason is that during the course of your season, some days you will feel strong and other days your body and hands will feel heavy and weak. As a result, it is mandatory during the course of the sea-son to change both the weight and handle of your bat as your strength ebbs and flows.

TIP: When your hands become tired, you will lose the feel. Change to a different handle and different weight to regain that feel. It will only be temporary. Once you get the feel back, return to your original bat.

> **TIPS FOR PROS:** When picking a wooden bat, look for a wide grain. If it's thin grained, the bat will splinter and crack more quickly. If it's wide, the bat has been made with the best part of the tree. If there are any knots in the barrel head of the bat, the bat has been made from the hardest part of the wood.

For the amateur player, aluminum bats come as long and light as you can handle. As a result, any batter can generate bat speed with an aluminum bat. Unfortunately for those of you with eyes on becoming a pro player, the aluminum bat gives a false sense of accomplishment.

One problem is that aluminum bat com-panies try to keep their bats light. It's diffi-cult to find an aluminum bat heavier than thirty-two ounces, and the light bat may pre-vent the batter from feeling the bat head, throwing off his rhythm and timing. You will not have the same feel using a thirty-five-inch, thirty-two-ounce aluminum bat as you would a similar wood bat.

As a result, an amateur batter with an alu-minum bat who becomes a professional and is forced to switch to a wood bat will need months to adapt to the different feel of the wood bat.

I recommend using the wood bat as much as possible in batting practice. The wood bat is dead weight; the aluminum bat is metal weight. Good bat speed is harder to attain with a wood bat, so by practicing with the wood bat you will strengthen your swing for the game when you use the aluminum bat.

Moreover, it is much harder to hit the ball solidly with the wood bat because you must hit the ball on the "sweet spot" in order for it to travel with authority. With the aluminum bat, the whole bat is the sweet spot. Even if you get jammed swinging an aluminum bat, you can get a base hit because of the bat's strength. Wood bats hit on the handle tend to splinter.

TIP: During practice work at the harder task, such as using a wood bat. That way, in the game your job will seem much easier.

CHAPTER 2

THE GRIP

The batter must find a grip that will give him explosive hands for maximum strength and bat speed. The position of the hands on the bat and the tightness of the grip determine the fluidity of the swing.

Gripping the Bat Comfortably

You first must grip the bat with the bottom hand. Here's how:

1. Hold the bat by the barrel with your dominant hand (right for righties, left for lefties) so the bat head is parallel to the ground and the handle is close to your body.
2. Place your nondominant (bottom) hand palm up with the elbow almost straight and the rest of the bat in that hand.
3. Release the barrel with your dominant (top) hand.
4. Your bottom hand should be able to maintain the parallel position without any assistance from the top hand.
5. The bat is held with the thumb and first three fingers of your bottom hand. Your little finger should be loose on the handle. A tight grip by your bottom hand will impede the wrist roll of your top hand through the hitting zone.
6. If the bat head drops, your bottom hand should move up the handle until you can hold the bat parallel to the ground.
7. Your bottom hand must keep the bat in a level position through your hitting zone.
8. Positioning the bat comfortably in your bottom hand will result in optimum

control of the bat head through your hitting zone.

Most batters don't pick the right grip. Basically, you have four choices:

1. Most batters, from Little League to the major leagues, mistakenly use the *end grip*. The pinky finger of the bottom hand grips the handle of the bat. I do not recommend this for anyone because it prevents freedom of movement by the wrists. The batter also has to force the top hand over, which brings the bat slightly up and over, causing a slight upward movement of the bat head during the swing.

2. In the *modified choke* the bottom hand grips the bat approximately two inches above the knob. This reduces the length of the bat resulting in a shorter lever, which allows the hitter to get the bat to the ball more quickly. The hitter sacrifices some distance and gains accuracy.

TIP: Use the modified choke when you have two strikes. You are in a defensive situation and need more bat control.

3. With the *complete choke* the bottom hand grips the bat a good six inches above the knob.

TIP: Use the complete choke if you are a spray or slap hitter.

4. The *overlapping finger grip* solves the problem of what to do with the pinky finger of the bottom hand. The bat has a knob on the end, which was designed to keep the hands from slipping off the

End Grip

end of the bat. The trouble is that the knob can be a real hindrance to the swing. The pinky of the bottom hand is placed on the knob of the bat and wrapped around. This will give maximum power, more wrist freedom, and a smooth path directly to the ball during the swing.

I recommend the overlapping finger grip for all power and alley hitters. The goal is to seek a grip that will free your wrists and allow a smooth, powerful swing. This is probably the one for you.

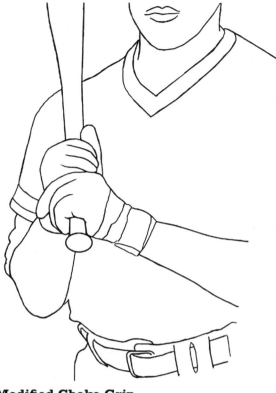

Modified Choke Grip

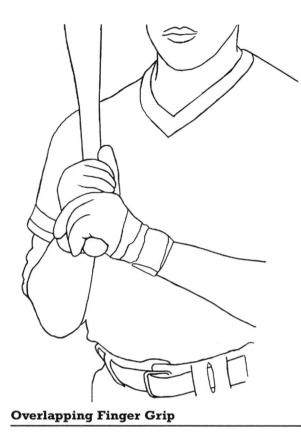

Overlapping Finger Grip

Lining Up the Hands

How should you place your hands in order to grip the bat?

As with most aspects of hitting, comfort comes first. The hands should be in a comfortable position. Gripping the bat is more than just placing hand over hand on the handle.

Reversing your hands—one facing toward the bat, the other facing away from the bat—provides maximum comfort. The important question is: how do you align the finger joints and the knuckles? There are two ways:

1. The preferable choice for power hitters, one I recommend highly, is to line the knuckles of the bottom hand with the finger joints of the top hand. This will give sufficient flexibility in the wrists and a firm grip.

2. For spray hitters who seek optimal bat control, I recommend lining the finger joints of the bottom hand with the finger joints of the top hand. With this alignment, the bat is primarily controlled with the fingers. As a result, the batter can't generate the power in the

swing as with the first alignment, but he will have maximum bat control.

How many times have you heard instructors tell batters to line up the knuckles of their hands? Too often.

TIP: Don't ever line up your knuckles. You won't have the flexibility OR the power to hit the ball consistently hard.

Position of the Top Hand

Your top hand grips the bat loosely with the bat resting across your palm. This allows the dominant (top) hand to rotate in the horizontal plane through the hitting zone. A

The Top Hand

tight grip on the bat with the dominant hand slows the bat barrel through the hitting zone.

Your top hand makes small and late adjustments as to the location of the ball. This allows you to make contact with the sweet spot of the bat through the center of the ball. Since the muscles making these adjustments are small, they require less time and can be made late in the swing.

Position of the Bat Barrel

Your top hand should be relaxed, with the bat resting comfortably in it. The bat barrel should be positioned at an angle between ninety and 180 degrees, depending on your strength and ability to control the bat head. You modify this position as the hands move down once the swing begins.

Holding the Bat

How tightly should you hold the bat?

So many times I've seen unknowing kids go up to the plate squeezing the bat as though they were going to reduce it to sawdust, but the tension in their hands, wrists, and forearms causes a slow swing. You have to relax at the plate. Any tension at the plate is counterproductive.

TIP: Hold the bat loosely so you don't create tension in the wrists, hands, and forearms.

Bat control is necessary for consistent hitting. If you don't have a loose grip, for example, you can't check your swing. A relaxed grip also enables maximum acceleration of the bat. If you are relaxed, your bottom hand

The overlapping grip

will pull the bat through the hitting zone, which helps extend your arms. The key to quickness at bat is getting hands to work together and making the swing a natural motion. The exception: hitting to the opposite field.

TIP: When hitting to the opposite field, squeeze your top hand hard on the bat. Here's why: to hit the ball the opposite way, your primary goal is to slow down the bat. The best way to do this is to introduce tension into your hands. If you do this, you will find it easier to go the opposite way.

THE STANCE

The stance is a firm foundation upon which we shape and mold the swing. The stance is the proper and comfortable placing of feet and hands in relation to the line of flight of the incoming pitch. It is a must to be relaxed and comfortable. It is a state where the body is at rest, waiting to begin an explosive movement.

Whatever stance you choose, you must be able to cover the entire plate with the swing of your bat. The stance must allow you to make contact with the sweet spot of the bat. You must be balanced while waiting for the pitch to arrive.

TIP: Hold the bat six to eight inches from your body.

If you hold the bat too far from your body, the swing will be long, leverage will be limited, and the coordination between hips and arms slightly restricted, causing a slower swing. If it is held too close, the effort is too great a push, making it impossible to be rhythmic and fluid. This, too, slows the swing.

TIP: Hold the bat up with hands at shoulder height and angled slightly back.

I know Wally Bachman liked to hold the bat pointing toward the catcher and Julio Franco toward the pitcher, but if you look closely, very quickly into the swing both batters had the bat in a normal hitting position at the time of approach to the ball.

It doesn't make sense for you to go to the extra effort they do. Wally and Julio mastered hitting and timing their way. But that doesn't mean it's right for you. It's so much easier to begin the swing with the bat in the proper hitting position.

COMMANDMENT 1

As you take your stance, bend both of your knees slightly and bend slightly at the waist.

It is impossible to be a successful hitter if you stand up straight at the plate. If you are standing up straight, you will not be able to see the ball very well. Anyone who hits that way is trying to hide a weakness. It's virtually impossible to hit a curveball standing up straight. Your head has to move so much you will have great difficulty tracking every pitch. You will be bobbing down to see the low pitch and most of the time you will be too late to hit it squarely.

If you bend your knees and waist, your body will be slightly above the ball as it comes to the plate. This will help you get your weight behind the ball. Notice that major league hitters bend forward.

TIP: If your knees and waist are bent, you will find it easier to go to the opposite field and make contact to all fields.

The bend at the waist is truly important for the purpose of balance and relaxation. If the batter is not relaxed, the swing will not be fluid. A hitter standing straight up is going to feel tense in the lower back and butt. A hitter bending over will have maximized his ability to relax.

Also, you have to get yourself in a position to obtain the best look at an incoming pitch. If someone is up on a hill and throwing a ball down at you, how would you get the best view of the pitch? If you're standing straight up, you'll see the balls pitched high in the strike zone, but not the balls thrown low. If you bend down, you'll be able to see both types of pitches.

Hall of Famer Billy Williams demonstrates the proper stance.

Crouching

While the hitter is in his natural stance, the strike zone extends from his armpit to his knees. The zone varies with the hitter's height and his degree of crouch.

TIP: Don't exaggerate your crouch.

Sometimes you have to exaggerate the crouch in order to disguise a weakness. However, an exaggerated crouch will make it difficult to rotate your body when you swing. Rickey Henderson is one hitter who exaggerates the crouch and has success, but notice that when he hits a home run, it's never down the left field line. He hits from alley to alley. Rickey can hit that way because he has extraordinary strength and a low center of gravity. His hips are locked, but he still can hit one out.

An exaggerated crouch usually will put the batter in a position to mess up all mechanics and will make it much harder to see the ball when it's pitched.

If you exaggerate the crouch and then swing the bat, you have to raise your body. As your body comes up, your head is forced to come up and move. If your head moves, the ball seems to move and is harder to hit. Since it's difficult to rotate your body, your swing will be slow and much of your power will be lost.

Foot Placement in the Batter's Box

The next decision you must make is where to place your feet in relationship to each other.

There are basically three types of stances:

1. The *straightaway stance* places both feet even with each other in the batter's box. There are two major problems with this stance: (a) the batter tends to open the shoulders too soon; and (b) his stride isn't toward the pitcher and the ball. Rather, the batter tends to step away from the ball.

2. The *open stance* places the back foot of the batter closer to the plate than the front foot. Certain batters like José Oquendo and Ernie Whitt preferred to hit this way. Rod Carew did, too, but there was only one Rod Carew. For most hitters, the problem with the open stance is that it only gives the batter a good look at the inside pitch. Outside pitches are very hard to hit with any consistency because the stride is away from the pitcher and the outside pitch.

The two main reasons a player uses a particular stance is to exploit his strengths or help disguise his weaknesses. For instance, if a batter prefers to hit an inside pitch, he will go up to the plate with an open stance. He'll crowd the plate, hoping the pitcher will give him something inside. A smart pitcher, of course, will realize what the batter is trying to do and pitch away. And a batter with an open stance will have great difficulty hitting the outside pitch.

3. The *closed stance* places the batter's front foot closer to the plate. The front side and the shoulders are turned in slightly toward the pitcher. Because the front foot is closer to the plate, the hips will be turned in properly, just waiting for the batter to begin his swing. Ninety percent of hitters in the majors today use a closed stance.

COMMANDMENT 2
Hit with a closed stance.

The closed stance gives you a firmer front side to hit against. It gives you the best balance, and when your front foot lands, your body stops and braces you, giving you the optimal power for the swing.

Most hitters, especially young hitters, have more trouble hitting the outside pitch than the inside pitch. The closed stance will allow your stride and momentum to take the bat toward the outside pitch better than any other stance.

The only negative to using the closed stance is that you become more vulnerable to the inside pitch if you have slow hands.

TIP: If the pitch is inside, shorten the swing and you'll still get the bat on the ball.

TIPS FOR PROS: The stance you assume is based on your hand, eye, and foot dominance. To determine foot dominance, ask yourself which foot you would use to kick a soccer ball as hard as you can. That foot is your dominant foot. To determine hand dominance, ask yourself which hand you use to do small, intricate work, like threading a needle or baiting a fish hook. That hand is your dominant hand.

The open stance

Use a closed stance when your dominant eye is closer to the pitcher or your dominant foot is the front foot. Use a square stance when your dominant eye is farther from the pitcher or your eye dominance is not established. Use an open stance when your dominant eye is farther from the pitcher and your dominant foot is the front foot.

With all stances, your body weight should be carried on the inside (big toe side) of your foot. This will allow you to utilize centrifugal force (force that is generated from within and moves outward).

No matter where the bat is positioned during your entire swing, your body weight should stay between the inside borders of both feet and should rotate around the axis of your vertebral column.

Foot Placement on the Plate

TIP: Place your front foot even with the middle of the plate. As you stride and meet the ball, hit it in front of you.

You want to be in command of the plate. You position yourself in the batter's box so that on the inside pitch the bat head will stay in fair territory as long as possible.

How often do you see a pro hit foul line drives one after another? The reason is that he is too far back on the plate. He thinks he will have more time to see the ball. But this thinking is not necessarily right. If he's that far back, he is giving the pitcher a lot more area to work with. He isn't taking command of the plate. He isn't saying to the pitcher, "Give me my part of the plate."

By the time this batter strides on the inside pitch and opens up, his hands are in foul territory and the bat head ends up pulling ball after ball into foul territory.

If the pitcher throws him a low, outside pitch, he will also have a problem. He won't make consistent contact with the ball because he's standing so far back he'll have to reach to hit the ball. He'll have to extend for full power—and then reach. If a batter has to reach, the swing becomes defensive and powerless.

How many times does the spray or choke hitter hit the ball into foul territory? Rarely. It's because he is up on the plate and his bat head is in fair territory. After the stride he's even with the plate and taking command.

If you start with your front foot even with the middle of the plate, you will be in the optimal position to hit breaking balls, split-fingered fastballs, and sinkerballs. This stance will take the low-breaking pitches away from the pitcher. He won't throw the fastball away. He's going to want to throw the fastball in on you.

Position from the Plate

How far from the plate should you stand? It can't be measured in feet or inches because the answer depends on the height and reach of each batter and his quickness and bat speed.

TIP: Position yourself to have good plate coverage so that when you swing, the barrel of the bat will go two to four inches beyond the outside part of the plate.

By positioning yourself for good plate coverage, you'll be better able to react to the pitch, whether it's inside or out, up or down. You'll be able to put the fat part of the bat in any location. Once you extend your arms and get the bat out across the plate, you'll know if that bat is covering the plate.

If you are tall with long arms, you will stand farther back. If you're short and use a short bat, you're going to have to get closer.

TIP: If you are a power hitter, stand farther back in the box, but only if you are comfortable back there. Henry Aaron and Joe Morgan didn't stand far from the plate. They were quick and hit a lot of home runs.

The Closed Stance

The front foot is closer to home plate than the rear foot. This stance allows the hitter to start from a coiled position. Power hitters find this stance increases the ability to explode into the ball with the hips and knees.

For the power hitter to hit home runs, he has to be able to pull the ball, and by standing back in the box, he's in better position to time the ball to pull it. Note that this is not easy to do and the downside is the large number of strikeouts.

For the young hitter, I recommend good plate coverage and hitting the ball to all fields. With the aluminum bat, anybody can be a power hitter.

Plate Coverage

To position yourself in the batter's box, know the length of your reach with the bat to

The Square Stance

The back foot is set first and can be dug in, with the toes squarely facing home plate. The front foot is then positioned at the same angle to the rear foot. The feet are positioned a comfortable width apart—far enough that a stable base can be maintained and not so far as to lock the hips and not allow them to rotate to the ball. The front shoulder rolls slightly inward (toward home plate) so the hitter can assume a coiled position.

You will notice that a lot of the power hitters stand back in the batter's box. They are back in the box because they try to get all their body momentum and weight behind the swing. Because their swing is going to be a little longer, they think they will have more time by being back in the box. They tell themselves the farther they are from the pitcher, the more time they have to take a strong, authoritative swing.

Plate Coverage

ensure maximum plate coverage. Follow these steps:

1. Place the bat parallel to the ground with both hands in your proper grip position.
2. Position your elbows and wrist in extension across the plate.
3. Assume your stance so mechanics of the swing are not compromised when making contact with the ball on the outside part of the plate.
4. Don't assume a stance so close to the plate that bat coverage extends beyond the outside part of the plate. You must also protect the inside part of the plate. To do that, on an inside pitch, keep your hands close to your body.
5. Stand deep enough in the batter's box to allow maximum opportunity to see the ball clearly and give you sufficient time to move the bat to it.

TIP: For power hitters, position your rear foot in the batter's box first. With arms and bat extended over the plate, a power hitter must best cover from the middle half of the plate to the inside corner. This allows you to pull the ball.

Head Placement

Position your head over your rear foot. Where your head goes, your center of gravity goes. Once your center of gravity moves forward, your hitting zone is diminished and your weight moves forward (toward the pitcher).

If your head stays back, your hands stay back. If your head moves forward, your

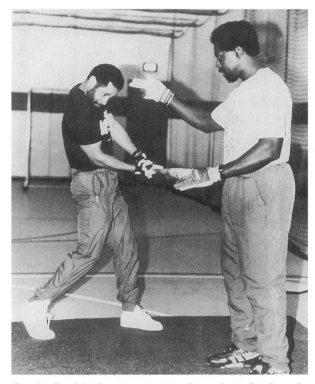

Ozzie Smith demonstrates keeping the head and eyes on the ball as you swing.

hands move forward. With your head still, you can judge the velocity, location, and rotation of the ball. With your head moving in the opposite direction from the ball, it is difficult to know where the ball is.

With your weight on your rear foot, the rotation around your back foot generates centrifugal force into your hitting zone. Once your head moves forward, the force generated by your rear foot, knee, and hip is lost.

Begin the swing with the chin in the front-shoulder area. End the swing on the rear shoulder on the follow through. This position ensures that rotation occurs around the

Chin on Front Shoulder

Chin on Rear Shoulder (Follow Through)

vertebral column with minimal head movement in any direction.

Weight Distribution

As you wait for the pitch you have a choice of keeping your weight on your back foot or evenly distributed.

TIP: Keep your weight slightly more on your back foot. You don't want to be too evenly balanced because you won't have a smooth weight shift backward, then forward. Your feet should be shoulder-width apart. This gives

you equal balance, an optimal starting point because you will be comfortable.

Recap

- Choose a bat that is comfortable and well-balanced.
- Place your pinky on the knob of the bat and wrap it around.
- Hold the bat six to eight inches from your body.
- Hold the bat up with hands at shoulder height and angled slightly back.
- As you take your stance, bend both

knees slightly and bend slightly at the waist.

- Hit with a closed stance.
- Place your front foot even with the middle of the plate. As you stride and meet the ball, hit it in fair territory.
- Position yourself to have good plate coverage so that when you swing, the barrel of the bat will go two to four inches beyond the outside part of the plate.

CHAPTER 4

THE HEAD AND THE EYES

COMMANDMENT 3

Keep your head motionless throughout the swing.

The head is located at the top of the cervical spine, and it is the axis of the swing. Like the earth that spins on its axis, the body swinging the bat rotates around the motionless head.

A motionless head keeps the hitter centered and balanced. Any excess movement of the head— either backward or forward—prevents you from executing a forceful swing. This is a big reason why the hitter with a big swing often makes less contact than the spray hitter. It's very difficult to swing hard and keep the head still.

TIPS: Any head movement will alter the arc of the bat. Head movement changes your line of vision and forces your eyes to readjust to the ball coming at you.

Your head controls balance because it is heavy. Move your head and your body will move with it. It is difficult to keep your head completely still.

Ninety-five percent of the time, when your head moves, it will move *away from the ball*. Mechanical flaws never take you in the direction of the ball. They take you away from it.

Most of a batter's flaws will be related to moving his head and front shoulder away from the ball. These include hitching, lunging, overstriding, pulling out the front shoulder, staying back too long, keeping the weight on the back foot too long, and uppercutting.

Tom Pagnozzi with his head positioned over his rear leg.

a stiff, rigid neck. It should be still, but relaxed. Keep your head down at the point of contact. Allow the momentum of the swing's follow through to force your head up from the area where the bat has made contact.

There is a common expression: keep your head down and see the ball. The problem is most hitters don't know what the words really mean.

TIP: Your head must be in a comfortable position, facing the pitcher in a slightly downward angle and following the pitch *into the strike zone.*

Once you've taken your stance, with your knees and waist bent slightly, in order to see the pitched ball you must put your head over the hitting area. In other words, if I held the end of my bat to my nose and dropped the bat, it would strike the ground on the inside corner of the plate.

If your head is positioned properly, your eyes will be able to see the plate when you are looking down and see the pitcher when you are looking forward. If you are looking out at the pitcher and the field instead of into the hitting zone, you will see the infielders and a wide spectrum of other distractions.

By lowering your head slightly and facing the hitting zone, you will keep your head still and move *only* your eyes to see the pitcher and his delivery. Nothing else will be in view to distract you. In other words, narrow your vision so you are concentrating on the pitcher and the incoming ball.

There is an old saying that you should watch the ball from the moment it leaves the pitcher's hand. It's impossible to see the ball roll off the pitcher's fingertips, but that doesn't mean you shouldn't attempt to see

What causes this movement away from the ball? The answer is universal: the desire to generate more momentum and power. In other words, if every major leaguer—including Mark McGwire, Jose Canseco, and Ken Griffey Jr.—kept his head motionless, he would be even more devastating than he is. But even major leaguers feel they have to sacrifice part of the mechanics to get that extra oomph behind the ball. I don't think so. It isn't necessary to hit a ball a hundred feet beyond the fence. They are so strong they don't need to sacrifice their mechanics to hit home runs, and neither should you.

TIP: As you take your stance, try to relax. One of the keys to hitting is to try not to have it. This makes your concentration much greater. Try to see the ball from the moment it leaves the pitcher's hand to the time it enters the hitting zone—*without moving your head*. As the pitch comes in, your eyes follow the flight of the ball. Your head remains stationary—until the ball gets close to the hitting zone. Then you will follow the ball laterally with your head and your eyes.

Every excess vertical head movement takes away from your vision of the ball. Each time your head moves up or down, the ball moves and you lose time and accuracy with the bat head.

There are three types of focus in hitting.

1. The *soft-center focus* is the wide range of peripheral vision. You can see the whole picture, the pitcher, the infielders, and the center fielder.
2. The *fine-center focus* concentrates on a small area, looking for details. You can see the stitches on the ball.
3. The *tracking focus* follows the path of the ball.

The untrained hitter will see everything out there. As you learn to focus first on the big picture and then concentrate on details such as the ball's stitching, you will find it possible to track the ball all the way to the hitting zone.

A player who does not hit consistently is one who does not see the ball consistently. Remember that concentration must be maintained. Without it, there will be sight but not vision. When you have vision, you track the ball all the way into the strike zone.

All the time coaches tell their players, "See the ball." But unless the batter has his head in the correct position for hitting and is in a position to concentrate only on the pitcher and the ball, such a general statement will have almost no meaning. No one can teach a batter how to track a baseball. It's a knack you acquire through time and practice.

TIP: Work on taking pitches during batting practice. Practice following the ball into the catcher's mitt. You must learn how to see the ball before you can hit it. Tell the pitcher you want to work on this so he won't be upset when you don't swing.

Proper Depth Perception

There must be coordination of both eyes. In other words, to hit well you must have proper depth perception. The lead eye will see the ball first, and with the coordination of the other eye, the ball will be followed into the strike zone.

You may not realize it, but normally one eye is stronger than the other. This is called the dominant or master eye. The master eye is the one that sees the ball best. As a batter, you always want the master eye to see the ball first. The master eye can send information to the brain 0.14 millisecond faster than the other eye.

For a right-handed hitter, the master eye usually is the left eye. For a lefty, it's the right eye. But unfortunately, it doesn't always work this way.

TIP: You can do an easy test to discover which is your master eye. Hold one hand extended six inches in front of your face, with your thumb and index finger in a circle. With both eyes open, look at the circle. Then close one eye. If the circle does not move, the open eye is the master eye.

Most batters enjoy cross-dominance—when the dominant hand and eye are opposite. But there are cases of left-handers whose dominant eye is the left eye and right-handers whose dominant eye is the right eye.

TIPS: If you do not have cross-dominance, you must compensate by turning your head more toward the pitcher. This will enable you to use your dominant eye to see the ball first.

Your eyes should always be on as level a plane as possible. This provides optimal tracking and focus on the ball.

You also must be aware that if you are a person who blinks a lot, you are at a disadvantage. The more you blink, the more your eyes appear to be going up and down. It is a distraction.

TIP: To decrease blinking while hitting the baseball, try opening your mouth as you swing. You will discover how difficult it is to blink with your mouth open. Eyes blink when they are relaxed. If you open your mouth, your muscles tighten and make blinking difficult.

A batter should never be told, "See the ball hit the bat." Instead he should be told, "*Try* to see the ball hit the bat." That's the challenge. It is possible to follow and see an outside pitch ten to twelve inches before contact. It's even harder to see an inside pitch. The speed of the bat and the ball prohibit seeing the actual contact.

TIP: Follow the ball with both your head and your eyes. Your head and eyes must follow the ball on the same plane as the ball. If you try to follow the ball with just your eyes, there will be a blind spot as the ball approaches the hitting area. In order not to lose sight of the ball, rotate your head back as the ball nears the plate.

COMMANDMENT 4
See the pitch five feet away and complete your swing.

If you have judged the ball's speed and direction properly, you will hit it. If not, you won't. The key is to begin tracking the ball as soon as possible and to see it as long as possible.

When I think of good eyes, I remember what I read about Ted Williams. He said good eyesight causes quicker recognition of the pitch, increasing the chances of making the proper adjustments in the swing and stride.

A hitter must be concerned with eye and hand coordination, eye movement, tracking ability, focusing ability, and reaction time. A hitter who has a visual breakdown will find it harder to concentrate and hit.

There are drills you can practice to improve your visual acuity. Don Mattingly, for one, spent hours working on his eyesight.

TIP: It is not possible to see the bat hit the ball and to take an aggressive swing at the same time. Therefore, you must sacrifice strength for contact. What is important is that you strike a balance. Being strong oftentimes can be dangerous because you may be tempted to swing harder than you have to, forcing you to take your eyes off the ball and miss more than you should.

José Canseco is so powerful he could hit a home run with an easy swing. But José always swings from the heels, and as a result, he unnecessarily prevents himself from seeing the pitch into the hitting area. Hitters must find ways to minimize losing sight of the ball. Cutting down on the swing, proper head positioning, and greater concentration are three primary ways of doing this.

Visualization

Visualization in hitting allows the eyes to control the body. Vision is partially muscular response to environmental changes in movement. As a batter you must learn to move your dominant eye in cooperation with the other, coordinate eye movement with head placement, and finally, coordinate eye movement with movement of the entire body. Once you can do that, stardom will be yours.

Recap

- Keep your head motionless throughout the swing.
- Keep your head in a comfortable position, facing the pitcher at a slightly downward angle and following the pitch into the strike zone.
- Track the ball from the pitcher's release point into the hitting area without being tense.
- Follow the ball with both your head and your eyes. Your head and eyes must follow the ball on the same plane as the ball.
- See the pitch five feet away and complete your swing.

C H A P T E R   5

BALANCE AND RHYTHM

Balance

Balance and rhythm are closely related because you can't have one without the other. In hitting a baseball, balance is mandatory. Balance is the key to hitting. Footwork is the key to balance.

Balance must be present before and during the swing and after contact has been made with the ball.

If you have balance, you will be able to execute all the facets of hitting in a smooth, easy manner, including going to the opposite field and hitting and running. It is also the key ingredient to making the correct weight transfer and getting the quick bat speed needed. Balance also helps remove all tension from the body. Hitting, fielding, throwing, and running all need to be done with balance and body control.

As I mentioned earlier, three of the keys to balance are:

1. spreading your feet comfortably apart
2. bending at the knees
3. bending at the waist

Movement throws off balance, another reason to keep your head still throughout the swing.

The knees act as an elevator. They can go up and they can go down. If the ball is high, you unbend and raise your knees to go after it. If it is low, you further bend and lower your knees to get to the pitch. Your knees get you into good hitting position.

TIP: If your swing is off and you are having problems seeing the ball, always check your balance. Chances are you are standing up too straight or have too much excess movement before the swing.

Rhythm

Rhythm comes from balance. Just as rhythm sets the beat of the song in music, so rhythm sets the beat of the swing in hitting. Rhythm is created in the hands before the stride. Rhythm begins the flow of the movement during the swing. Each hitter has his own rhythm. Like everything else, it takes work to find that rhythm. It's a feel you have to acquire.

COMMANDMENT 5

Rotate your wrists slightly in a continuous clockwise motion to set the rhythm.

Notice hitters who move the bat in their hands while waiting for the pitch. That's their rhythm. It's what they do so they won't be in a rest position at the time the pitcher releases the ball. Note in tennis the way players who receive the serve will rock back and forth in anticipation of the serve. That's rhythm. If there is no rhythm of the hands before the swing, the result is jerky motion and lack of gracefulness.

Notice that while a big leaguer is at bat, he's constantly moving his hands. The bat moves back and forth as he awaits the pitch. What he's doing is generating movement for the anticipated pitch. All batters should do this so they don't start the swing from a rest position.

TIP: There is a right way to set rhythm. Never move your hands in a circular motion, or up and down, because that will lead to a hitch, loss of bat swing, a late swing, and loss of coordination. Rather, slowly rotate your wrists slightly in a circular clockwise motion in preparation for the pitch. The head of the bat will make a circle about an inch in diameter. The movement should be so slight you aren't even conscious of it. At the same time, keep your hands still in a position of readiness.

COMMANDMENT 6

As the pitcher goes into his windup, turn your front shoulder inward toward the plate, which automatically will drive your hands and the bat backward, without moving your hands away from your body.

The hip and the knee will turn automatically. In essence, your entire front side should turn inward toward the plate. During the coil, do not pivot your lower body as in a golf swing.

Notice how Ozzie Smith turns his front shoulder in.

Ozzie Smith demonstrates the soft landing on the front foot.

Front Shoulder Roll

This brings the body into a coiled position which allows the greatest amount of force to be applied. This also ensures the hands remain back, enabling them to generate maximum force.

Now you are in position to stride.

Your upper body first pulls your lower body in this backward movement. When it is time to swing, the movement forward by your lower body will in turn lead your upper body. The result of this action will be excellent body rotation and superior bat speed.

There has been a misconception held by many amateur coaches that the initial backward movement is a movement of the hands going away from the body. DO NOT DO

THIS! If you first move your hands backward, you destroy all rhythm and make the swing long and slow, thus taking away all power. Remember that the object should be to get the bat into the hitting zone as quickly as possible.

The worst thing a batter can do is disconnect his hands and arms from his body. Obviously, this doesn't mean his hands and arms fall off, but the phrase has a very specific meaning in hitting: he has moved his hands back away from his body, forcing his bat to travel a much longer arc to get back to the hitting area. This results in a breakdown in mechanics and such flaws as his front shoulder coming forward too soon, his head focusing off the ball, and a long, lazy sweep of a swing.

Other coaches teach that the first movement in hitting should be forward. The problem with the weight going forward first is that you find yourself lunging because you become overanxious. Starting forward also takes the power away because there is no weight transfer behind the swing.

Stride

A stride is a way of starting the swing in motion. Your weight remains on the inside of your rear foot throughout, without a weight shift occurring on the step forward. Your front knee remains soft on the step. Your front foot is positioned with the toes pointed and the front knee slightly flexed in anticipation of a soft landing.

The pitcher goes into his windup. You go into the coiled position. The pitcher comes forward getting ready to deliver the pitch. Now begin your stride: your weight is transferred from your back foot to your front foot.

The stride does more than just allow you to meet the ball. It puts you in a waiting position so you can adjust to the incoming pitch and it puts you in position to have complete control of the bat.

The stride begins as soon as the pitcher moves his pitching arm forward. When that happens, you *slowly* bring your body forward in anticipation of the coming pitch. The stride moves the hitter toward the ball with power and balance.

The stride is only a gesture indicating you have prepared yourself to hit. When you stride, you are stepping away from your hands. You have to have good rhythm and timing for your hands to catch up with your body.

COMMANDMENT 7
Take a short stride.

It is important to take a short stride, six to eight inches or perhaps as much as a foot if you are tall and lanky. The longer the stride, the longer it will take the bat to catch up to your body. If your stride is too long, the ball will not jump off the bat because there will not be enough bat speed. The bat will be dragged through the hitting zone. A too-long stride will also cause you to end up on your heels, and the swing will become unbalanced. If your stride is too long, your hands will drop and you will swing in an upward movement. Uppercutting causes you to miss the ball more often than not because the bat isn't parallel to the ground and only a very small area of the bat can make contact.

With a short stride your hips won't lock and you can rotate your hands to your hitting zone. A short stride allows your weight to remain positioned over your rear foot to generate torque. The weight shift does not generate power. Power is generated by the rotation around the back foot, knee, and hip. Your stride has little to do with a weight shift.

A short stride is particularly helpful in hitting breaking balls and off-speed pitches. A short stride will also cause the bat to follow the hips. Suffice it to say that when the bat doesn't go forward soon enough, the hands, the least powerful of weapons, have to be called upon to supply the power and much power is lost.

TIP: If you see the pitch will be inside, your stride must be short so it can give your body a chance to rotate and get the bat head out in front of the plate. When you swing at an inside pitch, the bat must travel the longest distance. If the pitch is outside, you are allowed a little bigger stride because an outside pitch doesn't take as much time to hit. When the outside pitch is hit, the head of the bat will be closest to your body in the arc of the swing. Thus you can afford to sacrifice a little quickness in hitting the outside pitch.

A long stride increases your margin of error. It causes the bat to be slow. As with most things connected with the game, there have been players like Stan Musial and Roberto Clemente who had success with a long stride. But their particular genius was an ability to wait on the ball.

TIP: You should always take an aggressive step toward the pitcher.

COMMANDMENT 8
Stride softly.

Always land softly on the ball of your front foot. Step as though you are stepping on eggs. Land softly so your eyes can remain focused on the pitch. If you land too hard, your eyes will bounce up and down and you will lose sight of the ball in the middle of the pitch.

TIPS: When you land, always keep your hips loose because when they are tight, your body cannot move through the ball with the necessary power and speed. If you land hard and your hips remain tense, you will not be able to rotate when it comes time to swing.

Never land flat-footed. If you land flat-footed when striding, you will not have power in the swing and you won't be able to handle the outside pitch because your weight will shift away from the ball. If you stride properly and land on the ball of the front of your foot, your position will always be set for the outside pitch. You will be able to see the ball longer and still have power behind the swing.

If the ball should come inside, the proper response should be to roll the weight off the ball of the front foot and onto the outside part of the foot in order to open the hips and hit the inside pitch.

TIPS: Your feet must always remain parallel. This is necessary because your front leg should be the anchor which will stop your body's forward momentum and allow it to rotate with the swing.

If you are facing a fastball pitcher, your front foot must be placed in a hurry.

The stride must always come before the swing. It is impossible to stride and swing at the same time—the result is a lunge. You will commit yourself far too soon.

What it all boils down to is that you must stride properly to hit. Let me reiterate:

- Land on the ball of your front foot.
- Keep your front leg firm and straight because it is the anchor on which you will rotate and swing.

A number of excellent hitters, including Ruben Sierra, Matt Williams, Bo Jackson, and Danny Tartabull, opt to raise their front foot off the ground when they stride. For them, it's a timing mechanism. It pushes the weight back to the back foot. It gives them the opportunity to thrust all their body weight forward into the pitch. You are welcome to try this technique, but I must warn you that you'd better get your foot back down in a hurry in order to get yourself in the proper position to hit.

I once asked Matt Williams why he did this, and he said he felt he got extra weight and power behind the swing. If you can do this, and feel comfortable, go ahead. But be aware that you will lose some body control, and you won't be as well prepared to handle the outside pitch because you may find yourself out of position.

TIP: Your stride foot should not touch the ground until you have anticipated the location of the pitch.

You are now ready to hit the ball.

Recap

- Rotate your wrists slightly in a clockwise motion to set the rhythm.
- As the pitcher goes back into his windup, turn your front shoulder inward toward the plate, which automatically will drive your hands and the bat backward. Do this *without* moving your hands away from your body.
- Take a short stride.
- Stride softly.

THE ESSENCE OF THE SWING

Now we come to the actual act of hitting the ball. We combine the factors of eye position, bat position, weight shift, and placement of the shoulders, hips, and hands into one fluid motion consisting of different movements. The goal is the best possible swing. You must be able to react to any type of pitch with good results. To do this, you must understand and practice the fundamentals of hitting.

As the pitcher throws the ball in the direction of the hitter, the hitter's weight goes backward on the back leg (the cock), and the hitter's eyes are focused on the pitcher and his release point. The hitter's front knee is bent in slightly as are his front shoulder and hip. His hands are in a soft, relaxed position on the bat, and his body is balanced.

Once the ball has been sighted, he strides forward in the direction of the pitched ball to challenge it and react to whatever it does. His eyes continue to fix on the incoming pitch, and his head keeps as motionless as possible in the direction of the strike zone. As his brain anticipates the location of the pitch, his stride foot lands on the inside ball with his hands, hips, and weight held back.

COMMANDMENT 9

Once you see a hittable pitch, in a controlled and coordinated manner take the weight off your back foot and shift it forward, driving toward the pitch with your body.

TIP: Pick up your front foot. If your weight has to shift to your rear foot, then your weight isn't properly distributed.

Body Coordination

To attain optimal timing, the batter must coordinate his legs, shoulders, hips, and hands.

The Legs

The legs are the foundation of the swing. They start the forward body movement after the coil. They start the drive and put power into the swing. You can easily test this by standing with your legs close together and trying to swing the bat without moving them.

Leg movement precedes all other movement. The more your legs work, the harder you can swing the bat. Your legs move instinctively to get you into position to allow your body to rotate. They provide support for the upper body movement. They provide added power to the swing. If you use your legs correctly, you will take much of the pressure off your hands.

COMMANDMENT 10

Begin to rotate your hips BEFORE moving your shoulders and hands.

Just as the weight shifts from your back to your front foot, your hips lead your hands in an explosion of power with timed contact in the hitting zone. To accomplish this explosion of power, after the stride has been completed and the ball is in the hitting zone, your first movement is to twist your torso.

TIP: To twist your torso, turn your belly button to the ball. As your belly button moves, continue to hold your shoulders and hands back.

Ozzie Smith demonstrates the hip action of a swing.

In order to gain maximum power, your hips must rotate first so as not to block the freedom of movement in the rotation. Your hips must remain level at all times so your torso is rotating and not tilting, which forces you to swing up on the ball. If you are rotating properly, you will drive through the ball with the swing. You will be ready to unleash your shoulder and hands. This all takes place in a split second.

If you are not disciplined and stride too soon, you will have no power left to hit the ball. If you wait too long and don't stride soon enough, the ball will be past you and you will lose all power.

Proper timing will come from practice, practice, practice.

Rocking and Turning the Hips in the Coiled Position

Rocking can be used as a precipitating event starting the whole swing in motion. Rocking ensures that the weight stays on the inside of the back foot. The front foot comes to the toe with the front shoulder rotated to the rear.

COMMANDMENT 11

To create rhythm and movement, your first forward movement will be dropping your hands toward your body in order to be in the optimal position to hit the ball.

How far should you drop your hands? You don't even have to think about it. Just do it automatically. Your hands will then automatically raise back up slightly as you drive toward the ball.

When a person trips, have you noticed that instinctively his hands react downward

Horizontal Movement

Opposition promotes the generation of torque, which results in centrifugal force. Torque is horizontal movement around a vertical axis. Your vertebral column is the vertical axis which applies the torque at a right angle (force is applied horizontally to the ground).

Using the bottom hand to start the bat head down, bring the top elbow away from the body. This keeps the centrifugal force moving away from the center of the body.

to catch his fall? The hands react much quicker in a downward motion than upward. Rely on this same instinctive movement during your swing. When your hands instinctively move back up a little, you are ready for the forward surge of power.

TIP: During the swing, keep your hands close to your body.

If someone asks you to hold a fifty-pound bag of cement, do you hold your arms away from you or close to your body? You hold them close to your body because your arms are stronger when they are close to your body.

Keeping your hands close to your body also makes it easier for you to hit through the ball. If you start prematurely moving your hands away from your body, you will end up getting jammed if the pitch is inside, and if it's outside, you will hit around the ball rather than through it.

COMMANDMENT 12

Your bottom hand pulls everything into motion.

As you get ready to hit, nothing is forced. Hitting is a series of pulling and pushing motions. Your top hand is relaxed and your bottom hand pulls the knob of the bat forward, taking the bat head toward the ball.

COMMANDMENT 13

Your hands should always be above the bat head and the ball.

Moving the bat barrel into the hitting zone is accomplished with the bottom hand. The bat is gripped firmly with the bottom hand; the top hand is relaxed. The front elbow moves gradually from being bent at the start of the swing to extended in the hitting zone.

With the back elbow close to the side on the downward movement, the bat barrel actually moves away from the hitting zone. The barrel moves in an angle between 75 and 120 degrees. This allows the greatest velocity for acceleration.

The hands should always be above the bat head and the ball. They also should be in a cocked position ready to explode.

You always want to hit down and across the ball, even on the high pitch. You get the most power that way. The entire weight of the swing is going down across the ball.

If your hands are lower than the ball, you will hit harmless fly balls. Ted Williams was able to hit this way, but no one else could.

COMMANDMENT 14

As your hands approach the hitting area, your hands and wrists must be held back.

Your hands must be cocked and ready until you've committed yourself to swing in order for you to have force in the swing once you release your hands and your wrists. If

you lose control of your hands and allow them to move forward too soon, your hands will lose all their power.

COMMANDMENT 15

Don't commit your hands too soon.

Coaches advise, "Wait on the ball." But what does that mean to a hitter? It usually means to remain stationary until you see where the pitch is going. But if you follow this advice, you will find yourself in deep trouble because, if you wait that long, there is no time to execute a good swing.

A hitter who waits on the ball will inevitably start to apply the power of the swing too soon by beginning the swing too far back. The result will be a slow swing, loss of timing, pulling the head off the ball, and poor contact.

Instead of saying, "Wait on the ball," what he should tell you is, "Don't commit your hands too soon." Your body must be in position to hit the ball even before you know whether or not you are going to swing.

TIP: As the pitcher begins his forward motion to release the ball, you have to start moving your body slowly and cautiously in the direction of the pitcher, keeping your hands and weight back until you decide whether to swing.

It's like sneaking up on a chicken or rabbit and nabbing it at the last moment.

As the pitcher begins his motion and the follow through of his delivery to the plate, you will stride your normal six to eight inches BEFORE the ball arrives. The ball will arrive at the completion of your stride, and you will be in the right position to check your swing or to swing and complete your follow through.

COMMANDMENT 16

As you begin the swing, lower your front shoulder slightly and swing across the ball.

Ted Williams advocates a slight uppercut. Charlie Lau advocates a flat bat. Walt Hriniak favors releasing one hand from the bat on contact. For a select group of hitters, these recommendations might work. But for the greater percentage of players, to be a successful batter, I advocate the downswing.

If you drop your front shoulder slightly as you swing, this will cause the bat to drive through the ball with added force as if the

Chin Position on Front Shoulder

Resting the chin on the shoulder helps keep the head still and in the proper position to see the ball for the longest amount of time. With the chin on the shoulder, the hitter can focus on the release point of the pitcher with either eye (eye dominance will determine which eye tracks the flight of the ball). Also, it gives a driving downward feeling while hitting the pitch. If the chin is on the shoulder, the hitter cannot swing up.

bat head had been thrown at the ball. Keeping in mind that the bat starts out in the swing on a downward plane, as the swing continues it levels out to a flat plane, making it possible to hit the top or middle of the ball.

Many people think that when I say, "Swing down," you are going to swing the bat like an axe. Let me make it clear that the angle of the downward stroke is small. At the same time, the length of the swing is short. The combination results in better contact, greater bat speed, and incredible power.

Understanding that this is only the beginning of the swing, if there is any hope of hitting the ball squarely, the barrel of the bat must travel the shortest course possible. The bat head must cross the hitting area in the most direct line.

The downswing guarantees a horizontal swing and added power when the wrists are turned after contact is made. If the swing is correct, this occurs naturally. I look at the bat as an extension of my arms. The power travels the length of the bat as you swing. There is a transference of energy from the batter to the bat on contact.

If you uppercut, you tend to hit with your body, not your hips and hands. Also, when you uppercut, you can only hit the ball on one spot of the bat because of the angle the bat travels through the hitting area.

For the flat bat swing, the beginning of the swing leads to the bat head moving slightly upward, making it hard for the batter to hit the high pitch. By releasing one hand, you lose energy from the batter to the bat. Also, in doing this, the plane of the bat deviates uncontrollably once you release your hand.

COMMANDMENT 17
Throw the bat head forward toward the ball. DON'T swing the bat.

Using your wrists, throw the bat head at the ball. A hitting swing is a long movement. When you also swing the bat, you make the movement too long and lose timing and power. But if you throw the bat head at the ball, you achieve maximum bat speed and a good wrist turn.

As Ted Williams said, "To be a good hitter, to be quick in the hands, you must gain the maximum effort from the *wrists*."

Your wrists can only be used correctly when you understand how they are supposed to be used mechanically. If they are rolled too soon, there will be a mistiming with the bat head and the ball. Wrists are NEVER rolled. Good timing will come when your wrists turn over automatically with the momentum of the swing. Passively and reactively, your hands and wrists move automatically and take the bat head through the hitting area.

TIP: If you force your wrists to turn over, you risk turning them too soon and losing accuracy with the bat head. As a result, you won't hit the ball squarely and have good timing.

Though turning your wrists is passive, the act of waiting to turn them is not. As you wait, you must be in total control of your emotions and your body. The anxiety to move prematurely can overwhelm you if you aren't disciplined.

Waiting, like many hitting skills, is a knack. It is achieved by experience and practice.

The goal is accuracy of the bat head. It's like shooting a gun at a target. If you don't hit it, you're not accurate. Seeing the ball and controlling your hands produces this accuracy. Your concern should be that the bat meet the ball at the same angle every time. To do this, you must sacrifice strength of swing for feel and accuracy, and all your other mechanics must be intact.

The bat makes contact, then continues around your body as your torso rotates, and becomes a driving force as your weight and hips add power to the swing.

Billy Williams demonstrates the hand and wrist position to throw the bat head.

TIP: Your stride foot should be mobile and just firm enough to support hip rotation. If the knee of your stride leg locks too soon, you lose flexibility and you will not be able to adjust to the ball. Your stride leg becomes completely straight and locked *after* you make contact with the ball.

COMMANDMENT 18
Upon contact, snap your wrists and extend both arms away from your body.

This is called the follow through. This gives power to the swing and jump to the ball. It should be powerful and tension free. The follow through allows the momentum of the swing to continue without interference.

As your wrists snap in contact with the ball, the force of the swing and wrist snap will move the bat slightly to the front of your top hand.

TIP: Don't take your top hand off the bat.

This is another reason it's important to grip the bat loosely. If you grip the bat too tightly and don't allow the bat to move in your top hand, your swing will be constricted because of tension in your wrists.

If you are familiar with the teachings of batting coach Walt Hriniak, you know he recommends removing the top hand from the bat on contact. The reason is to prevent constriction of the follow through.

The problem with batting that way is you must concentrate your efforts to remove

Billy Williams demonstrates the raising of the rear heel in the follow through.

Both arms and wrists are extended just before contact and remain extended through contact. Extension increases the leverage for maximum application of force. The bat barrel is far from the center of gravity. It will move the fastest and with the greatest power through your hitting zone when acceleration culminates in extension.

your top hand from the bat, rather than hitting instinctively. And this swing will result in a loss of power because you are denied the power of using your top hand in the follow through. The follow through should be an integral part of the swing and should be terminated with power.

TIP: The follow through should cause your back foot to raise up at the heel, which permits the pivot and completion of the follow through.

The degree to which a player follows through depends on his level of flexibility. If the extension is good at contact, the follow through will be good. If the batter isn't flexible, the follow through will be weak. Will Clark, Rafael Palmeiro, and Tony Gwynn, for instance, have excellent follow throughs. Pete Incaviglia, Cecil Fielder, Steve Balboni, and the other muscular hitters do not.

Ozzie Smith demonstrates weight shift through the swing and raising the back heel in the follow through.

TIP: During the follow through your body should lean in the direction of the batted ball. This is evidence of good weight control. If the ball is hit to the opposite field, your body should be pointed in that direction. If the ball is pulled, your body should be pointed that way.

Follow through occurs after contact and is a gradual deceleration of body movements, resulting in deceleration of the bat head. The follow through does not affect the direction of the ball. This is determined at contact and cannot be altered after contact.

We have covered the essence of the swing from start to finish. Once you understand each component or phase of the swing, hitting a ball becomes much simpler.

Timing: When Bat Meets Ball

Timing is getting the body into the right position to hit the ball at the optimal spot on the bat.

Good pitching will throw off the timing of the hitter. Babe Ruth once said, "Hitting is timing and the turning of the wrists." Timing is the goal in the attempt to make contact.

It is impossible to have proper timing without the right bat. It is necessary to be able to feel the bat head in order to have a sense of timing. If the bat is too light at the barrel, you can't feel it and won't be able to direct it where you want it to go. Each individual swing is different. You have to create your own timing within your swing.

Timing is calculated motion—it should be an unconscious part of hitting. When you start to hit, you should follow your instincts. If you have to think, you won't be able to hit. Timing is like tying your shoes. Try explaining to someone how to tie your shoes without using your hands. It's impossible. Or try saying, rather than singing, "The Star Spangled Banner." It's impossible. No one can do it.

The simplicity of the hitting process demands that each factor of hitting be mastered. For timing to be right, your body has to respond in hundredths of a second. You have to coordinate your mind, body, and batting skills.

The point of the swing where both arms make a triangle is the point at your center of gravity where power is concentrated.

The swing should be an attitude of readiness, sureness of mind, and a single motion of eye, hand, and body. When a hitter's timing has been destroyed, his bat speed slows down.

It's very important that after your stride you are in good body position because this will afford you the opportunity to execute the beginning of a good swing. Your hips should be level so your torso can rotate. If your hips are not level, they are tilting, and you will come up and off the ball.

COMMANDMENT 19

Hit the ball when your weight shifts back to your center of gravity.

You make contact with the ball at the point where your weight shifts from your back foot to your front foot and is evenly distributed.

Maintaining body position is crucial during the swing and requires the center of gravity to be directly over your base of support—your feet. Yet, you must understand that your center of gravity shifts whenever you change position. If you lean back, your center of gravity goes back.

Each of us has a different center of gravity. Take Tony Gwynn and Dave Winfield. Gwynn will have a more consistent swing than Winfield because hitting is involved with movements close to the ground, and it is harder for the six-foot-six-inch Winfield to get down than it is for Gwynn.

You must find your optimal center of gravity in order to be balanced in the swing.

COMMANDMENT 20

The ideal location to make contact with the ball is somewhere in the zone between your center of gravity and the distance forward to your stride leg.

It is here where you generate the most bat speed.

This is not easy to do. The more often you can hit in this zone, the more successful you're going to be. If you can do this frequently, you're going to be a dangerous hitter. Remember in 1987 when Jack Clark hit thirty-five home runs for the Cardinals in half a season? Remember when Kevin Mitchell hit forty-seven home runs in 1989? That's what they were doing.

TIP: The goal is to make contact with the ball even with your front leg, which is just slightly in front of your body. If you make contact out past your front leg, most of your power will have been used up.

The point of contact will determine where the ball will go. For example:

- If you hit the ball in the arc of the swing closest to your body, the ball will be hit to the opposite field.
- If you hit the ball in the arc of the swing in the middle of your body, the ball will be hit up the middle in the direction of center field. This is where line drives are hit.
- If you hit the ball in the arc of the swing where the bat is farthest from the body, the ball will be pulled. This is what the power hitter strives to do. It's outta there.

How hard should you swing the bat? If you've done everything right, you won't swing the bat hard at all. If you swing the bat too hard, you lose bat control and accuracy with the bat head.

Meeting the Ball

Meet the ball in the center of gravity—in the middle of the body and slightly ahead, depending on where the pitch is.

At contact, body weight remains on the inside of the rear foot. Weight shifts after contact, and the momentum of the bat pulls the weight to the front foot. The front knee moves into extension just before contact.

The optimal swing is one with maximum speed *and* control. You must have bat and body control at all times. There has to be enough time in the course of the swing to fluidly execute every movement of the swing. You must start your movement as the pitcher begins his movements, and then gauge your movements as he begins to deliver the ball. If you've timed everything right, the bat will meet the ball squarely.

There's only one instant in the swing when you can apply this maximum effort with your hands. The two major factors are the speed of the swing and the speed of the pitch. If you reach for that maximum effort too soon, the swing will be long and you'll lose much of your power. If you wait too long, the same thing will happen. The key is to be aware of that optimal moment and attack. For this attack to be successful, you must be in total control. To gain this control, you must understand every aspect of the swing and work on any weaknesses.

If you think to yourself, "Swing easy," you will save the explosive movement for the right time and you'll hit the ball squarely. There will be a gradual buildup of speed through the swing, which will keep your fundamentals intact. Also bear in mind that for the optimal swing, you must give your hands time and room to swing. Every movement should be directed toward maintaining and gathering power in your hands.

Each correct movement is linked with and sets up the ensuing movement. In its entirety, the swing is a chain of actions, and when each part of the swing is done fluidly, it becomes instinctive—you react automatically.

Your Hitting Zone

Your hitting zone begins at the point where you swing your bat barrel down in a position parallel to the ground. Your hitting zone ends at the point where the bat barrel is no longer parallel to the ground. The total length of your hitting zone is about twelve inches.

The back of your hitting zone should be at the back part of the plate. With your head over your rear (dominant) foot, your hitting zone remains in front. If your head is positioned midway between your feet (front to back), you reduce the size of your hitting zone from front to back.

Your bottom hand moves down and forward from the top. This sets the back parameter for your hitting zone. Your top wrist rolls over to bring the bat head to the ball. When the bat head is no longer parallel, the front parameter from your hitting zone is established.

If you make contact anywhere in the hitting zone, the ball will be hit with maximum efficiency. The direction of the ball will be determined by the bat barrel position at contact with the ball.

As you become more aware of your hitting zone, you can narrow the parameters of the zone to fit a particular hitting situation (hit-and-run, sacrifice, fly ball, etc.).

Since the bat head moves in a vertical plane at the beginning, and the ball is moving in a horizontal plane, there is only one point in which contact with the ball can be made—where those two lines intersect. It is *impossible* to hit a high pitch with your bat parallel. For this reason alone, do not ever swing at high pitches.

Recap

- Once you see a hittable pitch, in a controlled and coordinated manner take the weight off your back foot and shift it forward, driving toward the pitch with your body.

- Begin to rotate your hips before moving your shoulders and hands.
- To create rhythm and movement, your first forward movement will be dropping your hands toward your body in order to be in the optimal position to hit the ball.
- During the swing, keep your hands close to your body.
- Your bottom hand pulls everything into motion.
- Your hands should always be above the bat head and the ball.
- As your hands approach the hitting area, hands and wrists must be held back (cocked).
- Don't commit your hands too soon.
- As you begin the swing, lower your front shoulder slightly and swing across the ball. The result will be a swing that comes down across the ball.
- Throw the bat head forward toward the ball. *Don't swing the bat.*
- Upon contact, snap your wrists and extend both arms away from your body. This gives power to your swing and jump to the ball.
- Hit the ball when your weight shifts back to your center of gravity.
- Try to meet the ball somewhere in the zone between the center of gravity in the middle of your body (in line with your head and belly button) and the distance forward to your stride leg.

PART II

Mastering the Mental Aspects of Hitting

CHAPTER 7

ZEN AND THE ART OF HITTING

"The groove is a calmness and a smoothness that occurs when you're having a good streak," said Kevin Bass, formerly of the San Francisco Giants. "Your timing is terrific, and you see the ball well. It's hard to be fooled because the movements in the swing are effortless. The body is calm and these factors bring on a great feeling of relaxation. I have that 'zoned' attitude, when I feel there is no one else playing. I can't be beaten because there is only me. Nothing sways or can defeat me."

Kevin Bass, when he was in his groove, was in hitter's heaven. He was Superman. He was in another world. This groove Bass spoke about comes to every great hitter at one time or another. It's what I call *the feel* and what you as a hitter should be striving for—your primary goal. In this chapter, I will discuss the mental factors which, combined with proper mechanics, can lead you to this nirvana.

It is important for you to understand that there are no quick fixes or magic potions to get you there. The first step always is mastering the mechanics, but after that you must search for the proper mental state in which to hit. If you do that, the grooves are sure to happen.

What I want my students to understand is that hitting is 50 percent physical and 50 percent mental. You must understand the correct mechanics, and you must know what to look for mentally. Controlling your mental outlook and your emotions is just as important as having proper technique.

"When I'm in my groove, I'm locked in. Nothing distracts me or dissuades me," said former California Angels infielder Johnny

Ray. "I seem to hit every pitch hard no matter who's throwing. I have a consistent, good swing. My feel is great."

The feel Johnny Ray spoke about is both a physical and mental experience. Imagine a sequence of smooth, uninterrupted movements with the absence of any conflicting notions in mind. Either the mind is free of thought, or whatever thoughts and notions are present are positive ones of harmony. This is a great feeling to have. The effortlessness of a correct swing is a sensation, a feeling. It seems so natural that when it happens, you wonder how and why it occurs.

A hitter hits a long home run, and his teammate on the bench says to himself, "He didn't take a very good swing. How did he do that?" The batter crosses the plate and comes into the dugout, and the teammate says, "You made that look so easy." The batter says, "I didn't really swing the bat hard. It seemed so effortless." The batter is perplexed.

The swing is in part a result of your emotions or feelings. Pick up a bat and close your eyes as though you are meditating, blocking out everything as you swing the bat. You can feel each movement of your body in action from start to finish. You can almost dissect it. This happens because when your eyes are closed, there are no outside distractions, so the feel of the swing is very prevalent. While you are hitting, your body makes ready for the actual pitch and the thought of the pitch. The action of the swing, if it is fluid, brings on a good feeling. The feeling from a good swing also is a great mental reinforcer. And if the swing feels agreeable, you will repeat it as long as the feeling lasts. Consequently, once you have discovered how important the feel is in hit-

ting, it makes it all the more necessary to find and keep those same movements that brought on the feeling in the first place.

When you have the feel, there is no anxiety. It doesn't matter who the pitcher is. There's no fear of failure, no tight muscles, no loss of concentration. You're in control. The timing is there. The movements are fluid. Your skill level is higher than normal. (I say higher than normal because you cannot stay at that level too long since distractions and flaws will appear sooner than you'd like.) Every movement is quick and forceful and accurate. You are performing within yourself.

When Pete Rose got his 4,192nd hit to beat Ty Cobb's record, it was a single. When Rod Carew made his three thousandth hit, it was a single. They stayed within themselves, doing what they did best. In these streaks the feelings are positive, and you enter the batter's box with high expectations of success. Everything happens automatically as though you're a tuned-in computer shielded from all distractions. You feel you have all the time in the world to respond accurately to the pitch. Your confidence is never higher. Success is not an issue. It seems natural and easy to achieve. The mind-body responds to your wishes. It's a trancelike state when you're at one with yourself and the physical world. Everything that's happening is instinct, and all your practice takes over.

As long as what you are doing at the moment is exactly that and nothing else—the mind is concentrated on one thing—confidence increases because you avoid dwelling on the past. When you dwell on experiences of failure in the past, your past will creep into your future. Your inner and outer focus must be solely on the present and not the future, where the possibility of failure is unlimited.

When you have the feel, everything happens without calculation or thinking. You are not thinking about how, when, or even where the ball is hit. You are not trying to hit the ball. You are trying to react to it, and how well you have made contact is not important. You are hitting in an automatic process without thought. There's always "sight of the ball" and "feel of the swing," but NO thinking.

If you can forget about intelligence and dwell on intuition, you can be free from anger and illusion and can focus fully on the present and eliminate all negative thoughts. Negative thoughts stimulate bad associations with the past and provoke negative concerns about the future.

It's not important to put a label on this process, though in Asian countries it's called *Zen*. Zen teaches one to lose the sense of self. You must have a noninterfering mind so you can respond to the present without interruption or deliberation. At the bat this produces quick, deliberate action in response to the sight of the ball.

This feeling also influences you to the point where, when it is absent, you try to garner it again. Just as the idea of how the swing should be performed is fixed, so the idea of the feel should be fixed.

Most hitters go to bat merely trying to hit the ball. The goal of the great hitters is to go to bat attempting to rediscover the feel. If they have ever experienced that feel, they look to re-create it. It's not enough for them to just swing and get the feel out of performing the swing. More important is to seek out and derive the tremendous satisfaction of finding that feel again. The great

hitters are always anticipating that feel, knowing one at bat soon it will come. You pursue the feeling for an entire season, knowing it is fleeting.

"When that good feeling comes and the base hits are falling, you know you have reached the point that occurs three or four times a season," said first baseman Cecil Fielder. "This is a time when a hitter is in his groove. Every time, the ball looks like a grapefruit. I see the ball from the pitcher's hand and put it in play. It's the time when the average rises.

"Mentally you have to have confidence, and with ability, good results come. Over the course of a season, your concentration level has to be good. In Japan, patience became an important element which I acquired playing there. In Toronto, I was a very aggressive hitter and swung at many bad pitches. In Japan, the pitchers throw all over the strike zone. Consequently, I had a lot of walks, but I learned to wait on the good pitch and that the walks come along with the hits. When you go up to the plate, you have to know yourself. Physical ability is not enough. Strength and a good head make for a good combination. You are just hurting yourself if you worry too much about your swing. Don't cloud your mind and think too much."

This beautiful, effortless swing you've taken is the result, not the cause, of a great at bat. Feeling is a perception, and because the movements used when hitting are the products and intent beforehand, there is this feel of effort. Movement, then, is the immediate effect of feeling.

The feeling you should be seeking will never come without a sense of purpose. As a human being, whether you have this sense of purpose is entirely in your control. Wishing yourself success in hitting is never enough. Willing yourself success is everything.

The factors that make up this sense of purpose are mental. The major components are willpower; visualization; concentration; confidence; determination, desire, and dedication; relaxation; patience and discipline; competitiveness; responsibility; and faith.

Willpower There must be a will to achieve. Will is not power, but at the same time, it is all the power there is. Willpower affects us physically and mentally while we are hitting. Willpower is an exercise of the mind over the body to do something positive, to complete a mission. The mind dictates, and the body follows. If you cannot concentrate, cannot keep a thoughtful moment, then your willpower has failed you.

Remembering back years ago, my first professional manager, Stubby Overmire, talked about desire. But to *wish* something to happen is incomplete. It's not strength of mind. However, when I say, "I will," this means something definitive. If you never tell yourself, "I will," then you have no will.

In action, it is will; in stillness, it is consciousness. Only an optimistic attitude can help develop will. It's like *The Little Engine That Could*. If you think you can, you can. A person may say, "I tried my best to concentrate, and I could not." It's not true that he tried his best. Your best does not end there.

To give your best means to gain fulfillment when the mind as well as the body are disciplined by concentration and willpower. They become your servants and work in your behalf.

Willpower is a commitment to move forward to accomplish a goal. This is the uncapping of the powers of body and mind through discipline and dedication. Confidence is a by-product of the hitter's belief in his own will. It takes on a power all its own. It is the foundation of all of our hitting endeavors. It affects more than thought and feeling. It affects performance. All the factors—reactions, balance of movement, coordination—are influenced by willpower. Willpower also has an effect on changes in the physical state.

Visualization Visualization is seeing into the future. You are seeing something you've never achieved. You look through your mind's eyes. Looking back can be inspirational, but in hitting you must always look to the present and think of the moment. We anticipate the bat hitting the ball. If you can visualize this occurring, your confidence will grow, your reaction time will be quicker, coordination and accuracy of the body and bat will improve, and you will get an idea of what will happen before you execute the movements.

If you can concentrate hard enough to visualize your at bats during batting practice, you will be able to visualize them in the game as well. This is imagination, created and controlled. The bottom line is that the goal is to achieve.

Visualization will influence your body mentally. It is the interworking of the brain connecting with the muscles and the muscles going back to the brain. There is no movement of any kind. It's just something you see in your mind.

Willie McGee has always said, "I visualize myself hitting a ball into the gap. It's amazing how often it actually happens in the game."

Visualize movement and motion. You do not want to visualize a still photo. See the actual movement of the entire swing, the follow through, hitting the ball—the full action picture.

Most batters seek to visualize a still photo. This is wrong. If you do not visualize action, there's no motion, and you can't do anything in any sport without motion. Motion is the essence of the swing. You're aiming to visualize your response to the change created by movement. So focusing on a still image usually results in failure.

Concentration   If you are confident, you're going to have good concentration. Concentration is the ability to eliminate all distractions except making contact with the ball. Pete Rose, Wade Boggs, and Bip Roberts demonstrate the importance of concentration.

Pound for pound Bip Roberts hits the ball as consistently hard as any player in the big leagues. This is a result of his intense concentration and the confidence it brings.

Concentration is a state of mind when the hitter is focused. You must have the ability to focus on a pitch without becoming tense—without being distracted by the pitcher's motion, leg kick, or any other movement in the area. Once you enter the box to hit, look at the ball in the pitcher's hand and tell yourself, "This is what I've got to see and hit." Concentrate on it only when it leaves the release point. You have tuned in your focus. You can see the pitcher's hand come forward, but you will not be able to concentrate on the ball until it is in flight.

The hitter's concentration should begin in the dugout, then continue in the on-deck circle and while at bat. Concentration must have a purpose for a particular at bat and must end once the at bat is over. You do not want your batting concentration to carry over to when you're in the field. You could end up getting hit in the face while thinking about your last at bat.

Concentration is pitch recognition, pitch location, and determining the speed and accuracy of the bat head. Concentrating on the pitcher's release point gives you an edge to read the pitch. In amateur and lower minor league baseball, some pitchers make hitting a little easier because they give away their pitches using different release points.

By concentrating, you can pick up the fastball release, which is over the top. The pitcher's hand passes near his ear. The curveball is released a little lower, the slider release is somewhere between the fastball and curveball.

The fastball will rotate from the bottom up because of delivery and the angle of the pitcher's arm. Sometimes the two-seamer fastball will be lighter in color than the four-seamer because less red will be showing. The curve has a downward angle of rotation and a rotation that is slower and tighter than the fastball. When concentrating to pick up the speed of the slider, look for a little red dot coming at you. Try to know as much as possible about each pitch.

Concentration thus is learned through practice and being able to control your focus.

Confidence   Confidence is knowing you are prepared to handle any pitch. This is a belief in yourself and your ability. When all thoughts are positive, you'll know exactly what you can do and what you can't do, and you'll be able to stay within yourself. In other words, you'll know just what you can do with the bat in your hands, and you'll do what you're capable of doing and nothing more.

Confidence breeds success, and success breeds confidence. You must know in your heart that you are going to get a hit every time you step up to the plate. Moreover, you want the pitcher to know you're confident. If he does, it will take away from his aggressiveness. It is something that can't be created out of thin air. It comes from being prepared.

Note that no amount of confidence will hit a solid line drive if the swing is improperly executed. A hitter with a solid swing who is not mentally ready will not hit as well as he can, but he will perform better than the hitter who has confidence but nothing to back it up. Psychology cannot overcome physics. As a result, feelings of confidence can be deceptive. But as a hitter, remember that true confidence is not a permanent possession because it can deteriorate in the presence of continued failure. The feeling of confidence is beneficial because it replaces feelings of insecurity and failure. You cannot have both at the same time, and it is certainly preferable to have the former.

The only confidence that is worth anything is the confidence that comes from knowing you have the skill to perform well. Yet, how you think you'll do depends a great deal on how you feel about yourself at the plate.

I have heard coaches tell other coaches concerning a player, "Confidence is right around the corner." I say it is as near as your next success. Your confidence reflects your belief in yourself.

Determination, Desire, Dedication
You can be skilled and you can have a perfect knowledge of the mental aspects of hitting, but if you lack the three Ds, which are all related, you will never be a great hitter.

Without constant practice and the willingness to put in a quality effort, your talents will only take you so far.

Your ability to hit will change constantly as your confidence ebbs and flows and your level of concentration increases and decreases. When you are feeling down, the only way to get back up is to get into the batting cage and hit two hundred baseballs until your confidence returns and your concentration level rises again.

The three Ds are essential to a hitter's improvement but they must be controlled. There is such a thing as being too determined. Some players try so hard they lose the ability to relax. And it is impossible to hit well if you are not relaxed.

Relaxation
Relaxation is the body at ease while the mind is in a clear, receptive state. You cannot force relaxation or command it. It is something that is acquired with time and experience. Confidence certainly is one key mental state to being able to relax because confidence knocks away the fear of failure. But relaxation also nurtures confidence. There are changes in the body and the mind when relaxation takes over. The brain waves and heartbeat are slower. Everything is in rhythm.

Relaxation allows the body and mind to discover their optimal balance. This balance improves physical performance and the inner feeling of confidence. Joe DiMaggio and Pete Rose, while they were locked into their famous hitting streaks, experienced this state of relaxation. They felt no anxiety or fear of failure while at bat, and I am sure they greatly enjoyed their streaks. How could it have been otherwise? I am certain that for at least one at bat per game, everything flowed smoothly.

Many hitters may experience such moments for one at bat or for several at bats during one game. But unless you can play the game with an absence of anxiety and fear of failure, it will be impossible for that feeling to last for anything but a short period of time.

A few years ago Willie McGee said to me, "Bernardo, I just can't relax." I said, "Willie, it's all mental. You must understand the difference between being aggressive and being anxious."

We know that to be a good hitter you have to be aggressive. This means you attack the ball when the right pitch comes your way. Anxiety is a state of uncontrolled preoccupation, a negative distraction. Anxiety clouds your ability to perform and forces your body to react prematurely.

I said, "Willie, an anxious mind cannot exist in a relaxed body because they are two opposites. When one is anxious, so is the other. When one is at rest, so is the other."

It was up to him to control that function within himself. So it is for you.

Many hitters go up to the plate too tense. They are the type of individuals who can't relax. They aren't comfortable because the situation seems too tough. They lack confidence. They fear failure. They put too much pressure on themselves to succeed. Or a manager or parent has put too much pressure on them to succeed.

These batters will execute an abnormal swing because of their anxiety. They care too much about the results and are preoccupied with those results. They may have a 2–0 count, and when the pitcher throws low in the dirt, they'll swing. It's a bad pitch to swing at, but they swing anyway because the mind has broken down.

Fifteen minutes before a game, you must relax. I tell major leaguers to pick up a bat and go into the outfield, swinging slowly and easily, trying to conquer the moment. You can sit alone at the end of the bench with your bat, clearing your mind, removing any distractions of life away from the ballpark. Take deep breaths and relax your body. You are putting your mind and body in relaxed readiness to hit. Being relaxed ejects the negatives.

Once you gain the feeling of relaxation, there will be a feeling that time is slowing down, but you still have a high degree of concentration and confidence. That's relaxation.

Patience and Discipline   Patience and discipline are virtually the same thing. Discipline is controlling your mind and reactions through training and experience. We control our actions, they don't control us. After being able to control ourselves, as hitters we must also be able to control situations.

For example, the count is 2 balls and 0 strikes, and Ozzie Smith is batting. A ball is thrown on the outside part of the plate. He will not swing because he's patient enough to know the count is in his favor and he can expect a better pitch.

Competitiveness   Competitiveness is love of the challenge of the pitcher-hitter confrontation. It is being aggressive under control. It's the batter with fire in his eyes. It's Pete Rose, Ozzie Smith, Bernardo Leonard. Give me my bat and get out of my way.

If you don't love the challenge, you will not rise to the occasion. You are beaten. You are lost. You always want to go to the plate looking to best the person on the mound. Competitiveness results in getting the job done. No matter what the pitcher is throwing, competitiveness allows the batter to reach deep down within himself to find the key to getting a base hit.

Responsibility   Every man is accountable for himself. Excuses don't cut it. You must make a commitment to yourself to perform at your best. I don't want more than your best, just your best. If you can look in the mirror and tell yourself you are giving everything you have, then the feel will come.

Faith   You must believe the feel will come. It's like the hero of the film *Field of Dreams*. He was told that if he built a ballpark, his heroes would come to play in it. He did and they did. It's that way with the feel. You must go up to the plate every at bat, anticipating that the feel will come. And one at bat, I hope soon, it will. And when it does, you will be in synch with the baseball universe.

"When I'm in my groove, it is total isolation," said Hubie Brooks. "I shut out everything, and I see nothing but the ball. When I am in one of those hot streaks, the ball always seems to be in a good hitting spot."

For the feel to come, you have to have a certain mind-set. It's a mental comfort zone. You must be in synch with your actions.

When you go up to the plate, it should not be with the feeling of "I have to hit," but rather "I want to hit." "Have to" is an obligation. "Want to" entails a lot more freedom and a lot less pressure. The feeling is always the overriding factor which determines success or failure.

Realize that the confidence you have as a hitter is directly related to the feel. The right feelings accompany the right actions. You can have the physical feel of the swing just by swinging the bat, but unless you also have the right mental feel, you aren't getting the true sense of the feel.

For instance, when you've played a game and hung out three or four line drives, you have the feeling of perfect control of the situation. This feel is also a feel of being in touch with your physical and mental strengths. The heights you reach in hitting should be attributed to how you feel inside. Feelings and emotions create energy and force. They trigger our psychological awareness. Oh, what a feeling!

Your hitting is an evolution and no end in itself. Everyone has a swing specific to that person. No other person has your genetic makeup, and therefore, your swing is as unique as your fingerprint.

Zen Musings

Elite athletes use rituals to become centered and focus on performance. These little external manipulations enable them to fix on what is appropriate so they can stay in the moment. To perform at your best, you must be conscious and deliberate. You must plan with forethought and remove your doubts and hesitations to focus on the task at hand. You must be composed, disciplined, and alert despite all that may be going on. This is awareness.

You are a visualizing entity. Imagination is your workshop. Thinking is the true business of life, and visualization is the result. The mind is real. Visualization is a specific technique that springs from your imagination. You actually create every detail of the future, calling into existence that which does not exist in the objective world. Regret of the past and fear of the future will steal your present. Concentration is much misunderstood. An idea of effort or activity seems to be associated with it, when just the contrary is true. You should be so interested in your thoughts, so engrossed in the present, as to be conscious of nothing else. Concentration does not mean the mere thinking of thoughts but the execution of thoughts.

Desire is the strongest motive to action; the more persistent the desire, the more authoritative the revelation. Your degree of success is determined by the nature of your desire. You will become more and be able to accomplish more. Every circumstance that exists in life is the result of some cause. All action is preceded by thought, and in the case of hitting, the thought is subconscious. Desire is the spiritual equivalent of gravity. It draws things together.

Attitude necessarily depends on what we think. Therefore, the secret to all power, all achievement, depends on our method of thinking. This is true because we must *be* before we can *do* and we can *do* only to the extent that we *are* and what we *are* depends on what we *think*. In order to express in life and hitting, we must think.

Nothing can exist without the mind. The mind is power, and most of our perceptions of power are external power, physical power. This form of power is based on limitation and is comparative. If one individual has power, then somebody else must be weak in comparison. As a hitter, you must have a mind-set with a power base that exploits the weakness of the pitcher.

This power is equally available to everyone. It comes from a personal harmony of thought, emotion, intention, words, and deeds. Your personal power is not controlled by the exterior. It is determined by how attuned you are to yourself and your personal improvement. The quality and consistency of thought is the cause of all effects.

Again, many say hitting is 90 percent mental and 10 percent physical. The mind is that vast mental storehouse where our thought processes originate. This tells us those who mentally prepare to achieve will achieve, and why all others must necessarily remain less than 10 percent efficient.

The subconscious mind never sleeps, never rests, any more than does your heart. It is the storehouse of memory, and hitting is all about muscle memory. The mind is a complex and wondrous tool. Use it. The mind acts as a recording device and is much better than any interactive CD-ROM. It takes in everything it is exposed to and replays any part when asked or stimulated. It interprets, attracts, and creates.

When you decide your hitting basics are sufficient, and you believe it, everything you see and hear will support that belief. The mind's ability to attract information is what allows you to improve. Not only artists and inventors use this creative ability of the mind; hitters do it all the time. If we expect nothing, we will have nothing. If we demand much of ourselves, we will receive the greater portion. We learn by doing. Through practice an athlete improves.

You must go within to attain control of body and mind. In the case of visualization you must believe it will come to pass. More, you must believe it already *has* come to pass. You must know it as reality. Without this belief, your goals are only a passing fancy, only wishful thinking. Believe it is done and you have claimed it. Belief, faith, and knowing will force it into existence.

The *I* in you uses the body as a vehicle and the mind for expression. The *I* controls and directs both body and mind. Just as what you fear will come to pass, what you have willed will come to pass. For this reason, it is best to always focus on what you want. In fact, it is wise to learn to live entirely without fear of failure in order to move forward.

The seeds you plant will be the fruits you reap. I can, therefore, I will. The most important conversations we have are the conversations we have with ourselves. They should be continual, as we are in our mindset of success. You can be what you will yourself to be. You can be what you choose to be. Please remember that no limitation can be placed on you by anyone but yourself. Nowhere is there any limitation. Everywhere is in abundance.

There is always the cry "to have" but never the cry "to be." People fail to understand that they cannot have one without the other. You must first find your kingdom before you can add things to it. You must accept responsibility for every at bat. You no longer can deny that you are the cause of your failures. You are the master of every movement of your swing and each emotion that comes with each at bat. The ability to eliminate imperfect conditions depends upon mental action. Our body is our mind and our mind is our body and it extends outside the body. This body-mind connection turns thought into the desire to execute, to create a concept of hitting and a feeling of comfort and confidence.

Concentrate on the notion that a human being is not a body with a spirit, but a spirit with a body, and for this reason, one's desires can't be permanently satisfied. Hitting, as we have said earlier, is like life. There are peaks and valleys. The power of attention is called concentration. It is directed by the will, and we must refuse to concentrate on anything except our desire to be mechanically correct. Concentrate on what you desire, hold it in your mind as a reality, visualize it in its completeness, and it will come to pass.

An earnest desire will bring about confident expectations and feelings. You do not achieve anything by affirming the opposite. If we are upset by anything external, the distraction is not due to that external thing but to our interpretation of it, and this you have the power to change at any moment. A man who is master of himself can end a sorrow as easily as he can begin a pleasure.

Hitting at something becomes habitual. So when you practice to develop your swing, make sure your mechanics are correct because you first make your habits and then your habits make you. Habits are either the best of servants or the worst of masters. The beginning of a habit is like an invisible thread. Every time we repeat the act, we add another strand, strengthening the thread until it binds us irrevocably through thought and act.

Character is not a thing of chance but a result of continued effort. To hit well, it helps to live an honorable life. Know yourself. Be aware of your limitations and always work to strengthen your weaknesses. To hit you must have peace of mind. So it is if you wish to live well. There are no shortcuts to hitting, as there are no shortcuts to life.

Confucius once said, "The essence of knowledge is, having it, to apply it."

Expect the best. Deserve it all. Go forth and prosper.

CHAPTER 8

IT'S A LONG, LONG SEASON

Slumps

Slumps are the result of uncoordinated movement and mistiming with the bat. Faulty mechanics will put you into a slump. Your mental state will keep you in it. No hitter is immune to slumps, though hitters like Tony Gwynn and Wade Boggs keep them to a minimum.

A slump occurs when the batter allows flaws to intrude in the swing, making the swing just a fraction slow. The hittable pitch you would normally hit hard is fouled off or missed. When you're in a slump, the tendency is to make your hitting worse than it really is. Your confidence suffers, your concentration lags, and your willpower fades.

When you're in the depth of a slump, it seems you can do nothing right. Your mind and body refuse to communicate. You will

not be able to consistently put the business end of the bat on the ball, no matter what you try to do. Even more depressing, you seem to send the few solid line drives into the gloves of the fielders. Other factors such as spectacular catches and bad calls from the umpires also hinder a hitter from reaching base safely. It seems everything is going against you.

As Tim Raines would say, "This is an unlucky slump." And when you are going through this, you even tend not to be able to remember those periods when everything fell in place. During slumps, your result does not match your effort. You try as hard as you can, but things just do not pan out.

When you have the feel, no one can tell you when a slump is coming. It may only take a game or just one at bat to head you in that direction. Personally, I believe it happens after a hitter has had a good streak, simply because a hitter can't go too long a period of time hitting the ball hard and consistently. So now comes a letdown.

Sometimes, when you're doing well, you tend to get too confident, too relaxed, and too cute. This is when the slump hits.

Since slumps are part of hitting and you know they are sure to come, you should be prepared to face them as calmly as possible. If a slump is prolonged, you put emotional stress on yourself that will affect your entire game. Being out of synch causes bad days.

There are real reasons for slumps: bad mechanics such as uppercutting, overstriding, hitching, not waiting on the ball, pulling your head off the ball, and trying to pull the ball at all times.

Making it worse is a negative mental attitude.

When you're in a slump and want to make a change, the first thing you must ask yourself is whether you're capable of making a mental adjustment. A lot of hitters can't do it. They can't divorce themselves from negative thinking.

Slumps are a state of mind. During this period you must have great concentration. With the mental and emotional factors in hitting, you can either get better or fall off the deep end. When a hitter begins to throw his bat or kick the water fountain, this frustration results in anger which cannot be expressed in any other way. He has lost his cool.

The fear of failure is both a cause and an effect of a prolonged slump. Putting stress on the hitter leads to a lack of production and exhausts and depresses him. Outbursts follow.

At times, oddly enough, knowledge can lead to a slump. If you feel you know a pitcher and can anticipate exactly what he is going to throw, you are tempted to try to hit the ball over the bleachers. You lose timing. A slump can begin.

Another slump enhancer is the shape of a particular ballpark. Fenway Park, for instance, is a common slump-starter for right-handed hitters.

Environmental conditions also have an effect on hitting, if emotional adjustments cannot be made. Try batting in Wrigley Field on a cold day and hitting the ball in on your hands. Your hands become numb and you may not be able to execute the proper swing for the rest of the day. Because you got jammed, you change your swing, but to no avail.

Wind conditions can start a slump. When the wind is blowing in, batters tend to overswing to compensate. You overswing and failure usually follows. Likewise, when the wind is blowing out, you try to loft the ball into the jet stream. You change your swing with poor results.

Because you face a different pitcher each day, you may find yourself off-stride if you don't adjust. That's why playing major league baseball is so difficult. The great hitter can make that adjustment every single day.

Excess cocking can also lead to and keep you in a slump. If you lift your front arm too far, forcing a too-long return, the result is a slow bat and a long swing.

All the faults and remedies have one common factor: timing. When all the coordination factors are in synch, the timing is right and the slump will end.

Batting practice won't necessarily get you out of a slump unless you are able to put yourself in the right frame of mind. You can be fooled during batting practice. In other words, you can feel great during practice, but once the game starts, you feel just as bad and play just as poorly as you did the day before. The reason: you are fooling yourself. In batting practice you can do almost everything wrong and still hit the ball because you don't have to anticipate and react. You know what's coming. It's important, then, to guard against yourself.

It's also possible to think you're in a slump when you aren't. You worry yourself needlessly. You may have made several outs in a row on great plays in the field, or you may have been overpowered by a couple of pitchers in a row. That doesn't mean you're in a slump. But if you convince yourself you are, you may put yourself in a slump that keeps you down for a couple of weeks.

Another thing you must guard against is being fatigued. The season is a long one, even in high school and Little League. You can't always feel in tip-top mental form. Some days you may feel tired. The bat may feel heavy. Your arms may be tired. So is your mind.

I have talked about the need for practice to eliminate mechanical flaws. But practicing provides one more important benefit: it will also help eliminate psychological weaknesses. If you have a good practice, during which you hit the ball solidly and everything feels right, it may change your mental attitude and get you out of your slump.

You must be self-aware and in touch with your feelings. The best remedy would be to take a day off, though I realize most players refuse to come out of the game no matter what. If you are like most, you'll play anyway. In that case I recommend: (*a*) looking closely at your mechanics by yourself or with a trusted teammate or coach, and (*b*) checking each of the twenty commandments and the other tips in this book to see what

you may be doing wrong. Your flaws will most likely fall into one of the following categories:

Problem   You are overstriding.
Result   You attempt to get something extra into the swing. You try to hit the ball long, rather than hard. The fear of a good fastball beating you may produce overstriding. Your front shoulder is so far out front that it locks your hips and affects your body's ability to rotate. You lack the necessary power because the contribution expected from your upper body is missing. You lose balance, which affects body control. You commit to the pitch too soon.
Cure   Lengthen the stride slightly to keep your head and body aligned with the pitch and make for easier tracking.

Problem   You are taking your eyes off the ball.
Result   You try to pull the ball with your body, making a jerking, sweeping swing. This causes your hips and shoulders to open too soon. You can't see the ball late in the hitting area.
Cure   Track the pitch into the strike zone. Wait as long as possible, keeping your head as close as possible to the swing. In this case, bunting is also helpful. In practice, take a normal swing after each bunt. The idea is to hit the ball in the same area where you bunted it. Playing pepper is also an excellent remedy to practice keeping your eyes on the ball. In pepper, a batter and a fielder stand fifteen feet apart. The fielder throws the ball and the batter hits a ground ball at the fielder, who throws it back again. The batter should take a short, normal swing. He should try to follow the throw to the contact point.

Problem   You are uppercutting.

Result   You try to pull the ball, and as a result, your front shoulder comes up and away from the ball, giving you a bad bat angle as the bat passes through the hitting area. There is less arc in the contact area. Most of the time the ball will be hit in the air, though once in a while it will go out of the ballpark.

Cure   Slightly lower your front shoulder. This will aid you in gaining a level swing. Lowering your front shoulder gives the bat approach to the pitch extra strength, and the feel of the bat barrel will be thrown into the pitch. The swing also will be much quicker and you'll have much more power behind it.

Problem   You are hitching.

Result   You drop your hands too much in trying to generate more power, and you raise them back to the hitting position in a circular motion. This causes a late, uncontrolled swing and loss of rhythm. The hitch is so much a part of the swing that you think this is the way it should be done. In adopting a stance, you must take care to overcome the fault. Hitching is also caused by excess cocking.

Cure   Relax your hands and slightly turn in your front shoulder. Your hands will move slightly back and not excessively down. Your head stays closer to your body, getting the bat to the proper hitting position more easily.

Problem   You are keeping your weight on your back foot too long.

Result   You can't pivot properly. This causes an uppercut in the swing, and your front shoulder comes off and away from the pitch. If you do this, you can't hit the outside

pitch and you lose power and body control.

Cure   *Step 1:* Bend your knees slightly. This will put you on the balls of your feet.

All these common faults, we must conclude, are associated with trying to get something extra behind the swing. Baseball is not one of those games where extra effort always pays off. This proves it.

Step 2: My magic slump breaker is a remedy I described earlier, a great aid to hitting the ball until you regain your confidence and feel: rest the bat on your shoulder. This removes tension and makes sure the path of the bat to the ball will be very short. You won't hit the ball with much authority, but you will make contact more often and with enough pop to get base hits, and base hits are what's needed to break a slump. Hit with the bat on your shoulder until you start to get your confidence back. Then go back to your normal way of hitting.

Step 3: Another remedy for a slump is to try to hit the ball consistently up the middle or to the opposite field. The attempt is to regain good coordination, good rhythm, and good timing of the bat on the ball. By hitting the ball up the middle and the opposite way, you give yourself a better opportunity to see the ball longer.

Step 4: Bunt more often. When you bunt, you must concentrate totally on putting the bat on the ball. If you can't bunt it, you definitely won't be able to hit it.

Streaks

It's only fair after talking about hitting slumps that we discuss the reverse, hitting streaks. When everything is happening just right, the line drives are jumping off the bats, and the jammers are falling, this is when we say the hitter is "locked in." He has the feel.

As I described in chapter five, you soon learn this feel is something you cannot possess. It comes to you temporarily, though some hitters can hold on to it longer than others.

Unfortunately, there is no way to prolong this feeling. Distractions come, like it or not.

The Golden Mean

Though I doubt the great poet Ralph Waldo Emerson ever played the game of baseball, he was the first to say that you have to smooth out the highs and the lows. His philosophy was to reach a golden mean, to never let himself get too high and never let himself get too low. His feeling was that you were never as well off as you thought and never as bad off as you thought. It's the same in hitting.

Whatever level you play at, nothing stays the same. You'll have your ups, and sure as can be, they will be followed by downs. How you handle these ups and downs emotionally will go a long way to determining how successful you are as a hitter.

BATTING PRACTICE AND MENTAL PREPARATION

Once you understand the correct mechanics of hitting, the next thing you must do to become a more proficient hitter is work on your deficiencies—in other words, practice until you have mastered each part of the swing.

Once you make the commitment to practice, it is important that you practice correctly. You should think about your game preparation before you ever enter the baseball stadium, and, in batting practice, you should begin to work on your game plan.

"In batting practice I execute my game plan," said Tony Gwynn. "My plan is to hit to the opposite field during the game, and that's the way I hit in batting practice. I believe that what is done in batting practice is done in the game."

Batting practice is an everyday process of creating an expectation of success. The extent to which you succeed depends on training your mind as you work in batting practice. We have developed physical training to a fine art, but we usually ignore mental training. Success as a hitter is not accidental. It comes from the quality time, dedication, and concentrated effort you give. Practice may not make perfect but it certainly makes for great improvement.

Practice is a time for working on your foundation for success. The game gives you the opportunity to test what you have worked on.

"During batting practice I will envision hitting against that day's pitcher and hit accordingly," said Ryne Sandberg. "If the pitcher is a breaking ball pitcher, in batting practice I will ask for more breaking balls and balls away. In batting practice I try to hit everything on a line or ground balls."

In batting practice, you should try to work within your capabilities and work on sound fundamentals. I have seen too many professional and amateur hitters who take batting practice for granted, swinging hard and trying to go for the distance when in games they may be slap or spray hitters. I can assure you these are not successful hitters.

"On my first turn in batting practice," said Ozzie Smith, "I hit the ball to the opposite field. I try not to overpower the ball. By doing this, I keep my front shoulder in, and it makes sure that I stay back on the ball."

You should work to the point where the movements are effortless and give a feel of confidence. This confidence is a large factor in the mental part of hitting.

Don't wait until you get into the batting cage to get loose. Batting practice is *not* a warm-up. If it is used that way, it is a waste of time. When you enter the cage, you should be ready to hit. This valuable time should be used to work on a sound swing, tempo, and rhythm. These factors are part of that elusive feel you are trying to achieve in hitting.

"My preparations begin in batting practice," said Willie McGee. "I visualize what I want to see happen. Sometimes I see myself hitting into the left field gap, and then it actually happens in the game."

During batting practice you must master the mind and body connection because you can't work on things when the umpire yells, "Play ball."

Former Chicago White Sox outfielder Dave Gallagher used to prepare himself by doing drills during batting practice. "Always try to have good swings in bat-

ting practice. You should never go into a game without having good swings."

A positive attitude will produce positive results. You learn about yourself and your capabilities. You should work and hit to the full extent of your capabilities and extend yourself to meet the challenge of being a successful hitter. Batting practice must be more than just standing there swinging a bat. You should spend that time relaxing and enjoying your time in the cage.

Practice is a very personal aspect of hitting and I'm sure routines vary. Nonetheless, if there are objectives, then they are purposeful. Batting practice puts your mind in gear for the game. But what's not simple is the exact nature of the exercise. To one person it may mean one thing and to another it may mean something else.

From day to day, series to series, the object of batting practice may change. It depends on the success and failure of the player. If I'm doing well, I will practice as little as I can. If I'm doing poorly, I will practice as much as I can. When you're doing well, you don't want to take the chance of having a flaw wander into your swing. When you're doing poorly, you will want to work to get rid of the flaws that have wormed their way into your swing.

You should be either working on staying in synch or trying to patch up a flaw in mechanics.

"I always think of the situation before I go to the plate to hit," said former New York Mets outfielder Hubie Brooks. "Mentally I consider the confrontation between myself and the pitcher as a battle. I must bear down and concentrate." Hubie would get ready for that confrontation in batting practice.

In batting practice, you can work on your timing, balance, rhythm, pivot, head stillness, and effortless swing. Where else can you work on your mechanical setup or the positioning of your feet in the stance? Only in batting practice. Where would we be as hitters without the time to work before we step into the fire?

Work hard on technique and build on your mental game. The tempo of practice should be the same as that of a game. You should value the educational impact of batting practice. Taking your swing for granted and losing your concentration during batting practice is a bad attitude to have in hitting.

As a rule, when you are physically tired or mentally fed up, slack up on batting practice for a day because a fault can creep into your swing if you suffer a letdown in concentration. Just remember, *never practice just for the sake of practicing*.

If for some reason I am unable to put in 100-percent effort in my practice, I am better off passing it up and coming back the next day. If your concentration level isn't up to par, you may think you're working to improve, but it will be illusory.

You should always practice with a definite purpose in mind, and when you accomplish it, try to refine it. When I'm pleased with my swing, I work on keeping it from getting rusty by rehearsing and repeating the fundamentals.

When you swing, always try hard to feel your body working so you have muscle memory to fall back on if your mechanics are off. When a fault has been identified, you must tackle it head-on. The good hitters like Tony Gwynn, Ryne Sandberg, Tim Raines, Don Mattingly, and Brett Butler remain proficient at their hitting game through constant work.

Practicing productively involves grooving the fundamentals that cause the swing and

reinforcing good habits. Practice also means having the guts to work on something new. But most of all, practice means putting in the extra time.

Practice pays off. It's the only way to cash in on the dividends of good hitting. It is the only place where you can study the flight of the ball hit in the air, the carry or the sink of a line drive, or the crispness of a hard grounder. The movement of the ball after you hit it tells you something about your swing.

Hit at a pace relaxed enough to permit you to feel and time the movements of your body and swing. When everything is right, the swing will feel effortless, especially during the forward movement to the ball. Try to make positioning your swing a reflexive movement. Practice is the single most important aspect of the art of hitting. This is where everything is rehearsed before the game actually begins. It is the single most important effort you can give in the preparation process. Putting in quality time will bring you the improvement you seek. The number of quality games you play during practice should outnumber those you play for real.

The cultivated swings of Gwynn, Sandberg, and Mattingly are not accidents. There is a reason those players are where they are: hard work.

As we train, working on our technique, we also train our minds. Our mental attitude will help determine how well we will play. In a way, I compare hitting with the lives we lead. We look for happiness through achievement and we spend our lives searching for it, always experimenting and exploring new theories and ideas. Success is often followed by failure in a never-ending cycle. You'll have difficulties, successes, and failures.

To explore, experiment, and experience is the true purpose of batting practice. Good hitters are confident in their training and practice, trust their impulses entirely, and don't have to think out every move. What the good hitter has done is make hitting simple and functional. Your aim should be to work day in and day out on basic hitting skills until they become second nature. Only when you accomplish this can you turn your complete concentration on the ball.

Every time you hit in practice, you should learn something. You should gain an experience. Your mind will acquire more hitting experiences than in a game simply because, when hitting in a game, there is only reaction time. There is no time to think.

In batting practice you should try to hit well. It is the opportunity to hit without pressure. If you don't work, you will find out it is easier to be worse than it is to be better. When you are lazy you tell yourself, "I don't want to be better." Hitting is a science, and you can never have enough knowledge about it.

Batting practice is also a place where suggestions and instructions can be worked on. It is vital to practice with concentration. Practice without purpose is worthless. Lackadaisical practice is inefficient and can be harmful. If you practice carelessly, an attitude of carelessness may enter into your hitting game. Incorrect movements may find their way into your swing without you even being aware of it. Be compulsive about practice. Be compulsive about wanting to improve. Work. Work. Work.

Your work habits will make or break you. If you never attempt to do things in practice, you will not be able to execute them in game situations. Practice is very valuable time. It is here that you build mentally, physically, and spiritually. These are the elements that together will produce the feel you should be searching for. You can accomplish nothing in the game until you can accomplish it in practice. We have been practicing all our lives and will continue to do so. It's a never-ending process.

Mental Preparation

When you go up to the plate, you must be mentally prepared and conditioned. It's a reinforcement of positive thinking and attitude adjustment. Mental preparedness is having some preknowledge of the pitcher. You have to do some homework before you walk up to the plate to face that pitcher.

Mental preparation begins way before the ball game. The great player takes advantage of batting practice, and he also uses his wait in the on-deck circle to learn as much as he can about the pitcher he is about to face.

The good major league hitters all prepare for the at bat. Here's what some of the best have to say:

Tony Gwynn

Before I step into the batter's box, these five questions come into my mind: What does he throw? Is there a pattern to his pitching? When he's in trouble, what pitch does he rely on? What kind of success have I had against him? Does he work around me or does he work me carefully?

It's very important to know the pitcher. I prepare for each game by reviewing videos of previous games. I study myself versus opposing pitchers.

Ryne Sandberg

Mentally my preparation for the game starts

with knowing who is pitching and then thinking about the pitches that I might see.

Dusty Baker

My mental preparation begins before I arrive at the ballpark. In the on-deck circle I observe and study the pitcher. I look for his best pitch and his pattern. I try to pick up the pitcher's weakness.

Since the on-deck circle is the closest spot to being in the batter's box, visualizing myself adapting to the situation is very important. Will Clark is very good at anticipating the pitcher's next strategy. He is studious and he prepares well for the game. Pitchers have different release points—overhand, three quarters, sidearm—and it is important to know them. I study and observe pitchers because it is not good to be fooled by a pitch I did not know he had.

Tim Raines

In the on-deck circle, I check the ball's velocity, and the break on the curveball, and whether the pitcher is throwing high fastballs or low breaking balls.

George Scott, who was a star with the Boston Red Sox and Milwaukee Brewers, kept a journal on all pitchers' strategies against him. He always arrived early at the ballpark so he could observe and prepare himself mentally for the game.

George Scott

When I was in the on-deck circle, I never worried about how the pitcher pitched the batter before, simply because we were different types of hitters. I would look for pitch location. Was his fastball inside all the time or away? I wanted to know how much his curveball was breaking.

If a pitcher threw a certain pitch with control frequently, sometimes I would intentionally take

that pitch for two strikes, waiting for the pitch I wanted to hit.

Johnny Ray

In the on-deck circle I study the pitcher to see which pitches he throws, and I think about how he will pitch me. Each club has scouting reports, and I adjust to how I think he will pitch me, according to our reports.

Kevin Bass

When I'm in the on-deck circle, I am observing what is happening on the field. Questions come to mind: Who's on base? Who's batting behind me? Is it a double play situation? Whenever I lead off an inning, I want to be aware of the score. All these factors are important for me to consider.

Hal McRae

Positive mental thinking is necessary while in the on-deck circle. I visualize what's going to happen. It's positive reinforcement for me. I have already told myself what the alternative situations are and what I'm going to do when I get up to the plate. I always try to have a plan of attack with successful thinking.

Dwight Smith

In the on-deck circle I look at what the pitcher is throwing, know his outpitch, know what he threw to the batter ahead of me if he is a similar hitter.

These men each may be looking for something a little different, but basically their approach to the game is the same. They want to be mentally prepared. They want the greatest advantage possible when they go up against the enemy—that day's pitcher.

As a batter you also must have some knowledge of the catcher. Tony Oliva, the hitting star of the Minnesota Twins, once told me, "By having knowledge of both, sometimes you will be surprised, not all the time surprised."

It's possible to be on the same wavelength with the pitcher, but if the other team has a thinking catcher, you have two men lined up against you.

A catcher will call the game. He is closest to the batter. He can see whether a batter makes an adjustment. His job is to pay attention to where and how close to the plate you are standing.

Whether you are playing Little League, Pony League, or major league baseball, use batting practice for improvement. Use it to strengthen weaknesses or to practice what you feel you're going to come up against in the game.

And when you're waiting in the on-deck circle, watch what the pitcher is throwing. See where the ball is going, at what speed, and with how much control. Be smart. Think like the pros.

Here are some questions you ought to be thinking about before you step into the batter's box: What is my task and my objective during this at bat? What kind of stuff does the pitcher have? How many different pitches does he throw? What type velocity does he have? If he is overpowering, I must be exceptionally quick with my hands. If he isn't, it gives me the luxury of laying back and being more patient. What is his best pitch? What does he throw when he's in trouble? How much success has he had against me, and I against him? If he is much more successful against me, he has an advantage simply because of his prior success. If I have been successful against him, my confidence will be high, but I will have to watch out for overconfidence.

The goal is to prepare in advance of the at-bat. Then once you arrive at that plate for the job at hand, you must clear your mind and let your reflexes take over. Anticipate the feel.

GAINING AN EDGE

All hitters look for an edge, an advantage. Most batters believe they need to have an edge on the pitcher. That can happen, but it is important to understand that the edge you go up to the plate with more often comes from your state of mind. It's your belief that a particular piece of knowledge is going to help you. Here is some information to study and internalize, useful ways of thinking to give you an edge at the plate.

Hitting is easiest when you swing at pitches in the strike zone. When you swing at bad pitches, you're making your job tougher.

A pitcher never really tries to throw a strike. He wants to throw the ball near the plate, around the plate, at the edge of the plate in an attempt to get you to swing at a pitch you won't be comfortable swinging at. The pitches that most often get you out are the ones that look hittable but aren't.

If you only swing at pitches over the plate

and in the strike zone, you will have an edge. To do this, you must work hard on your discipline—know the strike zone. Swing only at pitches you can handle. Patience and discipline will force the pitcher to throw you a better pitch. You will never become a good hitter until you learn the strike zone, know your weaknesses, and try to keep the pitcher from throwing in those areas. Knowing the strike zone and not being disciplined enough to hit strikes is worthless.

Hitters like Roberto Clemente and Yogi Berra were exceptions. They could get the fat part of the bat on the ball no matter where the ball was thrown. They created their own strike zone because pitchers could not come up with a strategy that would consistently get those batters out.

The secret to becoming more disciplined: practice, hard work, concentration.

THE SUPERSTAR HITTER'S BIBLE

Within the official strike zone, you must be able to define your own personal strike zone. In that personal strike zone, you have to know which pitches and in what location you hit best. If you can hit the high, inside pitch but can't hit the low, outside pitch, you're going to have to swing at the former but lay off the latter—until you get two strikes.

Wade Boggs knows the strike zone exceptionally well. Ted Williams knew it better than anyone. It was said that if Hall of Famer Rogers Hornsby took a strike, the umpire surely would call that pitch a ball. Hornsby literally forced the pitcher to throw him something he liked because the umpire knew his reputation for a keen eye.

By developing a good eye, you will not swing at a pitch around the plate, but only those over the plate. No matter what the pattern of the pitches, you must make sure the ones you swing at are strikes.

When you're standing in the batter's box, you should not view the pitcher as the enemy, but as someone who is standing out there on the mound for your purpose. The pitcher throws as fast as 90 MPH. He's exerting a lot of effort. You, as a hitter, don't have to work very hard. You swing easy, and the ball will go out of the ballpark.

A batter without a pitcher can do nothing. If he doesn't throw the ball, you can't hit it. He is someone whose strengths when joined with yours create a result in your favor. The relationship between the pitcher and hitter exists in the moment. Look at the pitcher as though he is dependent on you. You don't want to fight him. Rather, you should be analyzing his strengths and then using those strengths for *your* benefit.

If you say to yourself, "That guy is working *with* me," you will be in a far better state of mind than if you see him as an opponent. He's out there because you *need* him out there. And when you hit one out, don't forget to thank him.

Good hitters see what they want to happen, and the below-average hitter fears what might happen. The mental game is about being optimistic. You must be able to accept what you can do and what you cannot.

The lack of proper warm-up causes an early sensation of fatigue because the body has not been prepared for the amount of work to be done. This is why I respect the pinch hitter so much. He comes up to hit without warming up. He must get loose during his first swing.

Swing enough before the game so that when you get up to the plate for your first at bat, your first swing will be one of your best.

Somewhere in the hitting process exists the word *luck*. It isn't physical or mental. It's the third part of the puzzle in hitting. But be aware of the saying, "Luck is the residue of design." Those who work hardest tend to have the best luck.

Luck is prevalent. When a Texas Leaguer falls, that's luck. A long fly ball lost in the sun is luck. So is a bunt when the pitcher forgets to cover first base.

In hitting there is no such thing as bad luck. You can hit a hard line drive right at someone. It's caught. But you've done your job. You've hit the ball hard.

You have to believe in yourself, but that belief must also be realistic. There is a foolproof technique inside the mind, the power of positive thought. As simple and nonscientific as it may sound, thought separates champions from average players. The technique is called motivational rehearsal. I call it mental rehearsal.

Long before the game is to be played on the field, you should play it over and over in your mind. If you think about many different outcomes, there can be few surprises when you get on the field. You will have seen it all beforehand.

Mental rehearsal combined with physical practice produces a large edge in your favor. You have the advantage because you've been there before, if only in your mind.

Although mental practice does not make perfect, it does make permanent. The idea is there, if not the success. Assuming mental rehearsal is repeated consistently, in time it creates permanence.

Every successful hitter has his own consistent style in the way he thinks. He keeps it simple. The hitter for average tries to do one thing: make good, solid contact. The home run hitter wants to do one thing: look for a ball he can loft and send a good distance.

In hitting you don't *make* things happen. You *let* things happen. Once a hitter tries to make things happen, there will be pressure on him to *do* something. When you're at bat, your job is to *react*, not to *do* something. That's because you are not in control with respect to where the ball is thrown. You can only hit what the pitcher gives you. That's your job as a hitter.

Breathing is a key element in relaxation. It is very important to inhale and exhale deeply at the plate, in the dugout, in the outfield—any time you begin to feel tension or anxiety or doubt or distraction. You want to try to breathe it away. You must inhale and exhale to the full capacity of your lungs. This is the way babies breathe and the way you breathe when you're asleep. This is a quick and very effective way to relax.

Step out of the batter's box, take a deep breath, and come back rested and fit.

You must try to find a conscious control that will take the place of thinking. Otherwise anger, frustration, or other emotions will get in the way of a restive state when you get up to hit. Buddhists pick a syllable to chant in order to rid all words, thoughts, anxiety, and other negative emotions from their minds.

I don't believe you can think and hit by feel at the same time. Feel is acquired through repetition of muscle memory, and thinking inhibits muscle memory. The feel of the swing will be there no matter what your mental state. Mental state is part of your preparedness. You don't use it once you step into the box. So if you're thinking, you're in trouble because all that preparedness will be clouded and won't be available to you.

Muscle memory gives you a nice, forceful swing. The swing itself is outside the mind. Any control that's within the mind is vulnerable to state of mind and is unreliable. Nevertheless, you as the batter must adjust to each pitch. That is within your mental control.

Obsessions work against you. If you are obsessed with getting a clean base hit, the mind's mental computer will be concentrating on getting on base successfully when it should be obsessed with the thought of making good contact. Your concern should be executing the necessary movements to make a good swing and hit the ball as solidly and consistently as possible. These movements are controlled by feel, and one should be conscious of the feel. I call this psychophysical equilibrium. Everything has to be under control, which should always be a primary goal in hitting.

Why can a batter have good swings when there's no ball coming at him? When a player swings in the mirror or in the on-deck circle, the swing is so easy and smooth, it looks nearly perfect. In game situations the swing changes with the added element of the ball.

Knowing the ball is coming or just seeing the ball will upset the batter and affect his swing. When the batter sees the ball, he has the obligation to hit it. It's another reason not to make hitting the ball your goal. Good contact and follow through should be your goal.

Hitting is difficult because your body, which is your source of power, is never in line with the flight of the incoming pitch. The only way to be aligned with the pitch is to be behind it, like the catcher or umpire. The body is on either side of the ball so the production of power must result from body rotation.

The mind knows how it is going to swing the bat, and though the thinking may be flawless, the execution of the swing may be incorrect because the physical ability to execute does not measure up to the mind's conception of it.

The mind can put pressure and strain on physical ability. If you find this happens,

back out and try to relax. Gather yourself, not your thoughts.

As the ball nears the plate, it slows down slightly. It doesn't pick up speed—I don't care what anybody says. A lot of batters think they have to hit the ball before it reaches the plate because they are afraid it will speed up as it travels through the strike zone. This is not the case. The ball actually slows down a fraction when it reaches the plate. It may not be measurable with the naked eye, but it does slow down. You can tell just by standing behind the pitcher and watching him turn the ball loose. As it enters the hitting area, the ball moves. Any movement is a result of the ball slowing down.

If my approach to hitting is only to make contact, I don't care if the pitcher is throwing the ball 90 MPH. All I have to do is wait until the ball gets there and put my bat on it. The batter who hits with power won't wait. He'll try to attack it, which causes error in contact. Putting the bat on the ball cuts down on your margin of error. A pitch can't be a strike until it gets past you. You're guarding the plate. Say to the pitcher, "This plate is mine. Let's see you throw it past me." You don't concede anything to any pitcher—ever. The plate is yours. It belongs to you.

Expectations are dangerous in hitting. All players say to themselves, "This year I'm going to hit .330 with twenty home runs and 100 RBIs." Their realistic expectations usually are below their goals because most players inflate what they wish to do. Such planning is very dangerous and foolish because it tends to bring players disappointment and anxiety.

You should never put pressure on yourself, and expectations give you the opportunity for disappointment. Expectations are a form of self-promotion, but inflated expectations cause great problems because the chance of failing becomes greater.

If you don't have a track record, don't set goals. Let the possibility of your achievement be limitless. If you set a goal at ten home runs, once you hit the tenth home run, you may inhibit your success because in your mind you'll have accomplished your goal, even though you might be a hitter who ought to be bashing twenty home runs.

When a pitcher has good stuff and control, your best chance of success lies in trying to hit the ball where it is pitched. If you try to jack out Roger Clemens, and he keeps throwing the ball away, you're in trouble. You have to go with the pitch.

Never go to the plate looking to take a base on balls. This takes away from your aggressiveness. Be selective. Take the walks if the pitcher gives them to you. A walk is as good as a hit. When you're ahead in the count, mentally you should narrow your strike zone. Tell yourself only to swing at a pitch over the heart of the plate. If you consistently look over the middle of the plate, every hittable pitch will seem to be in that area. If the pitcher is ahead of you, you have to widen your strike zone and be more aggressive.

If an opposing manager puts on a shift against you, he's not trying to defense you in that particular area. Rather, he wants to get you to hit where you ordinarily don't, taking you out of your game and making you do something you're not as comfortable with.

A manager will usually call for a shift in a home run situation. If you have the ability to control the bat, hit to the opposite field. If you don't, ignore the shift and go for the downs. Teddy Ballgame was criticized for not hitting differently against the Boudreau shift. Teddy was right. His critics were fools.

Stubby Overmire was my first minor manager in 1973. He told me to turn the label a quarter of a turn and hit with the part of the bat where the grains run. "This is the hardest part of the bat," he told me. He also told me that during the course of the season, when you are feeling tired, hit with the label toward you—the bat will look shorter because the label breaks up the continuity of the grains.

If you want the bat to look longer, turn the label away. It's the same bat, but mentally it's a different look. And if a bat looks shorter or longer it'll feel shorter or longer. It's an illusion, but one that gives you an edge.

Keys for Improving Your Hitting

Nine Keys to Hitting the Fastball

1. Time and execute a quick swing.
2. Place weight on your back foot.
3. Keep your eyes on the ball.
4. Start your front shoulder in. Your back shoulder will move forward and down.
5. Your wrists and hands should be the only parts of your body moving in the instant before contact.
6. Your hands should be level as you make contact.

7. Keep your head down.
8. Roll your wrists after contact.
9. Follow through after contact.

Four Keys to Hitting the Breaking Ball

1. Keep your weight back and under control.
2. Be patient, wait, and follow the break of the ball within the hitting zone as long as possible.
3. Keep your head down on the ball.
4. Maintain a normal, consistent swing.

Six Keys to Hitting the Fastball to the Opposite Field

1. Follow the ball with your head.
2. Ease into the ball and make early contact, hitting the ball slightly behind your body with your top hand slightly tensed.
3. Keep your hips open slightly, allowing for clearance.
4. Keep your hands behind the ball.
5. Keep your hands level on contact.
6. Roll your wrists during the follow through.

Two Keys to Hitting the Breaking Ball to the Opposite Field

1. Wait on the ball longer, and delay your forward movement.
2. Keep everything else the same. Try to keep the same consistent stride.

Pulling the Ball

The pull hitter hits his share of home runs because he hits down the line, the shortest part of the ballpark. This comes with experience and hitting the pitch in a certain area or zone. The hitter puts the bat on the ball in front of the plate and in front of the body. He has a longer rotation as he puts all his weight and effort behind the ball. The more rotation, the more force and weight behind the swing. The ball is hit later. The swing starts slow and then you explode out in front of the plate.

Six Keys to Being a Good Hitter

1. You must have a need to improve, succeed, and excel.
2. You must have dedication, patience, and discipline to training. Condition yourself to achieve.
3. You must have the willingness to compete without holding anything back.
4. You must be able to practice and compete without being pushed by someone else. Self-motivation is crucial.
5. You must be willing to acquire more knowledge and not be intimidated by new ideas. Evaluate new ideas and how they can apply to you.

PART III

Overview

THE STARS RAP ABOUT HITTING

I have had the pleasure to work with some of the finest batters in the game. As you will see, each player has different things he is concerned with, believes in, and works hard to improve. It proves what I have been telling you: like snowflakes, every batter is unique.

Tony Gwynn

I try to keep hitting simple and basic. My approach to hitting is similar to that of Harry "the Hat" Walker, who often said, "You see the ball and react to it."

Patience is a virtue. Stay back on the ball and let it come to you. If you rush out at the pitch, you shorten the distance between the mound and the plate.

A groove is what I call my zone. I really don't know how I get there, but I feel certain things before I arrive in the zone. Once I am in that zone, it is a great feeling. Usually I hit one pitch—I may take a pitch or two, but when I swing the bat there is usually good, hard contact. The one I hit is hit hard. I don't worry about who is on the mound today or what pitcher will be on the mound tomorrow. When I am in my zone, my confidence level is sky high.

Before I step into the batter's box, five questions come to mind:

1. *What pitches does he have?*
2. *Is there a pattern to his pitching?*
3. *When he is in trouble, what pitch does he rely on?*
4. *What kind of success have I had against him?*
5. *Does he work around me or work me carefully?*

It's very important to know the pitchers. Since I have been in the league a while, I feel I know them pretty well.

I prepare for each game by reviewing videos

Tony Gwynn

from previous games. I study myself and opposing pitchers. In batting practice, I execute my game plan. My plan is to hit the ball to left field, my opposite field. This makes me stay back and wait for the ball.

I believe that what is done in batting practice will be done in the game. After the season ends in October, I begin hitting on November 1. During this period through December 31, I hit about three days a week with two hundred swings per day. During the time from January 1 until spring training, I increase my number of swings from three hundred to about five hundred per day. In the three weeks before spring training, I try not to use the batting machines because they have a tendency to make me jump at the ball before it is seen. The quicker the ball is seen, the better the

chance of hitting it. I do not lift weights, but I did do dumbbell curls to strengthen my injured hand.

Ozzie Smith

A player should determine what kind of hitter he is going to be by looking at his own limitations. I try to be a consistent line drive hitter. I use my eyes and legs to get on base and to make things happen. I strive for a good on-base percentage. I believe that good techniques are essential in being a consistent hitter. It is important to quiet the lower body and utilize the hands.

I use a line drive swing which starts down and levels out as the bat head moves through the ball. In order to drive the ball, good techniques need to be used. A quick, short, and compact swing is a good swing. On my first turn in batting practice, I hit the ball to the opposite field.

Ozzie Smith

By doing this, I keep the front shoulder in, and I try not to overpower the ball. There is an instinctive, natural reaction to the inside pitch. I try to use the whole field in preparation for the game itself.

When I'm in my groove, there is no thinking, and everything just happens. The technique is quick, natural, and consistently correct. If I begin the swing correctly, I will finish correctly, but if I begin the swing incorrectly, I will finish incorrectly.

The most important aspect in my hitting is the start. While I am in the on-deck circle, I am mostly thinking about using good technique. My goal is to hit the ball consistently hard. As long as my setup and approach are correct, I can usually achieve this.

I mentally want to do something positive in every game—either get a big hit, move a runner over, hit a sacrifice, or anything to help the team. Whether we win or lose, I want to do something positive.

I believe the good years of a player happen when the team has the good years. The guy in front of me and the guy behind me play important roles. The guy in front of me sets the table.

Matt Williams

I try to stay inside the baseball, meaning to hit the inside portion of the baseball, not the outside where you pull and hit the ball hard, but into foul territory, wasting a hittable pitch. I am not a pure hitter, and I am an aggressive hitter and sometimes get in trouble because of it. I try to see the pitch from its release point. I do not look for a certain pitch, nor a certain location. I look for good pitches in the strike zone and try to hit to all fields. When I think of driving the ball I look for a pitch to pull, and if the pitch is otherwise, then I am forced to take what the pitcher has given me.

Matt Williams

When I am hitting the ball to all fields, and when I'm hitting the ball hard wherever the pitch is thrown, I am in that groove. My stride is an aggressive one. It looks as though when the pitch is coming, the ball seems to stop for me. My concentration level is tuned in. There are no outside variables in my head. I have good balance and good control of my swing and my bat.

Every major league player has the physical talent, but the mental part of hitting is tough to conquer. Mentally, I tell myself to pick up the ball, try to recognize the pitch, and hit it hard somewhere. The body does what the mind tells it to do.

In the on-deck circle I try to time the pitcher's fastest pitch. I can do this while the pitcher is warming up or when there is a hitter ahead of *me. With the Giants, I had an advantage hitting behind Kevin Mitchell because we are both pull hitters. Basically, they pitch us both the same way. If the pitcher would start Kevin off with a fastball high and in, usually it would be the same pattern for me. So I always watched closely what the pitcher threw to him.*

My open stance began in spring training because I had a problem stepping in the bucket. This gave me the chance to make an aggressive step in the direction of the pitcher. It also helped me to keep my hands inside the ball. The high lift of my stride foot is not something that I worked on. I just started doing it, but it gives me leverage and power in my swing. I believe that expectation may have an effect on the good year turning to a mediocre one. Human nature is to improve, but to expect too much is fatal. The large contracts, pressure from oneself, from the media, the fans, and merely trying to do too much is distracting. Try to do the same things every day. Our bodies are muscle memory machines.

Ryne Sandberg

Ryne Sandberg

My approach to hitting is simple and basic. I try to see the ball all the way to home plate. I want to hit the ball on a line and go with the pitch wherever it is. I use the entire field.

When things are going well for me, when I'm in that groove, first I see the ball well, then my pitch recognition is good, and I am well balanced up at the plate. I try to put the good part of the bat on the ball, consistently making good contact. I find that I can handle the pitch that's in *and the pitch that's away, resulting in good plate coverage.*

Mentally, my preparations for the game start with knowing who is pitching, then thinking about the pitches I might see, and last, knowing his best pitch. During batting practice I envision hitting against the game-day pitcher and I hit

accordingly. If the pitcher is a breaking ball pitcher, in batting practice I ask for more breaking balls and balls away.

To the young player I would recommend getting a bat that you can handle. Get one that's not too long or too heavy. Select a bat that you can swing with authority. Have a stance that's comfortable and balanced. Try not to have too much excess movement in the swing. All good hitters have a short stride. The shorter, the better. The swing should be somewhat level or down. Always try to hit the top of the ball. Hit line drive base hits or hard ground balls. In batting practice I try to hit everything on a line or on the ground.

I don't think that any one thing outvalues any other. First, see the ball all the way in. Keep your head on the ball. Second, keep the stride short.

The short stride helps in keeping the hands back better. If you can keep the hands back, you can hit.

The good years can turn to mediocre years when injuries hamper the swing. Or you can have a mediocre year after a good year because the pitchers go after you much more carefully. If you do not adjust, then the result will be negative. You must adjust. Teams may have scouting reports that tell pitchers to pitch you differently. Sometimes bad starts and an early struggle will lead to bad habits and change your swing. Always try to be steady and consistent.

Cecil Fielder

My approach to hitting is to look for the fastball. I am a fastball hitter, so I try to concentrate on my strength.

When that good feeling comes into play, and the base hits are falling, you know you have reached a point that occurs three or four times a season. You're in a groove. Everything looks like a grapefruit. I see the ball from the pitcher's hand and put it in play. That's the time when the average rises.

Mentally you have to have confidence. And with ability good results come. Over the course of the season your concentration level has to be high. I learned patience in Japan. In Toronto I had been a very aggressive hitter, swinging at many bad pitches. In Japan, the pitchers throw in the strike zone. Consequently, I learned to wait on the good pitches and began getting a lot of walks.

When you go up to the plate you have to know yourself. Physical ability is not enough. Strength and a good head make for a good combination. You can't afford to sit and think a bit and worry about your swing 'cause then you won't get base hits. Be patient and be selective.

In giving tips to younger players, first let me point out that we are all different. If there is a

Cecil Fielder

norm, make sure of the position of the feet in the batter's box and make sure the hands are in a comfortable position. Let let them have fun and do what's comfortable.

Once you have that good year, the pitchers pay attention to you and throw you more difficult pitches to hit, pitches in and away and not in the middle of the plate. For you to get good pitches, the hitter behind you has to hit.

Bobby Bonds

Good hitting starts with good balance. In the stance, the weight should be 70 percent on the back leg and then rise to the 50 percent level as the weight moves forward. Let the hands come first and the body follow. If you commit the body first, you will have bad balance and your swing will be bad. Try to see the ball leave the bat and always hit the top half of the ball. Work to the

Bobby Bonds

Tim Raines

The rhythm and weight shift are important to my way of hitting. I hit up the middle and to the opposite field. I hit the ball where it is pitched. Many batters look for a certain pitch or look in a particular location, but I only look at the ball. My approach is the same on every pitch, and that is to be aggressive. I am ready to explode on the fastball. Against the breaking ball, I keep the hands and weight back.

When I am in a groove, I can hit any pitch that anybody throws. I don't have a tendency to swing at bad pitches. A good hitter will take walks until a good pitch comes along.

I prepare mentally for each at bat. I don't look ahead at my next at bat, and I don't look behind at my last at bat. I focus on the present.

point where your swing is consistent. The bottom hand is your power and pull hand and the top hand is your speed and guide hand.

Work the hands and eyes in unison. The hands react to what the eyes see, and the body always follows the hands. Patience is very important. A relaxed hitter is a good hitter. You are quickest when you are relaxed.

Mental confidence and a certain amount of arrogance is important. A person who doubts himself is a defeated person. When you are in doubt, negative things happen. Arrogance is believing in yourself. Arrogance is mental toughness and a strong mental approach is necessary. You have to understand that one negative will destroy ten positives. No one ever beats you. You only have an off night. When there is doubt, there is room for error. All the great hitters have a certain arrogance about them.

Tim Raines

88

Willie McGee

I believe in seeing the ball and hitting it. I try to stay within myself. I want to remain in the strike zone and hit the ball hard. It is important to be aggressive on the pitches in the strike zone.

When I am in the groove, I know I will hit the ball three or four times a game. It's an inner confidence. Everything is ready, and I don't think or worry about mechanics. It doesn't matter who is pitching. I am relaxed, and it is a feeling I wish would last a long time.

My preparation begins in batting practice. I sometimes picture myself hitting into the left field gap and then it actually happens. Injuries and domestic problems turn the good years into sub-par. It can be anything that interferes with your concentration. Injuries are the biggest reason.

Dusty Baker

I try to keep my hitting as simple and natural as possible. I want to be properly balanced and relaxed. I concentrate on seeing the ball leave the pitcher's hand, keeping my head down on the point of contact, and keeping the bat on the same plane to the ball as long as possible. It is important to start slow and explode into the ball.

The mental preparation for the game begins before I arrive at the ballpark. The best mental approach is to have good concentration. In the on-deck circle I observe and study the pitcher. I look for the pitcher's best pitch and his pattern. I try to pick up on any weakness. Since the on-deck circle is the closest spot to being in the batter's box, visualization of myself adapting to the situation is very important.

Will Clark is very good at anticipating the

Willie McGee

Dusty Baker

opposition's next move. He is studious and he prepares well for the game. Pitchers have different release points for their different pitches, and it is important to know the differences. I study and observe the pitcher so he won't fool me with a pitch I didn't know he had.

Brett Butler

My hitting philosophy is to take my time, see the ball as long as possible, and react to it with the shortest possible swing.

Ty Cobb once said hitting is $33^{1/3}$ percent ability, $33^{1/3}$ percent concentration, and $33^{1/3}$ percent luck. I don't believe in luck. For me, concentration is the most important factor in hitting.

I try to study the pitcher by watching a few pitches during my first at bat. I look for certain pitches, but while I am hitting it is in my sub-

conscious. I study tapes of opposing pitchers and look for the velocity of their pitches. Pitchers do not throw the same way every time, so I try to hit the ball hard as many times as I can.

Hard work is the key to success because nothing comes easy. Work on the negatives and constantly practice the positives.

Mark Grace

Hitting has to be a pressureless process. I try to have a good at bat by not swinging at bad pitches. I look for a good pitch, and I hit it. I am relaxed, confident, and always try to hit the ball where it is pitched, from foul line to foul line. I focus on the pitcher and his release point. I don't think too much, and I am not superstitious. I try to stay relaxed, loose, confident, and carefree.

Brett Butler

Mark Grace

Danny Tartabull

I try to make contact with the top half of the ball, use the left- and right-field alleys, and I try to stay away from the left- and right-field lines.

I believe in hitting to the opposite field. The battle begins in the on-deck circle. That's where I make my preparations. I try to have a plan. I prepare myself mentally by doing extra work, thinking positively, and believing in my ability. To combat the bad years, I try to maintain my level of concentration.

Tom Pagnozzi

I want to be selective and wait on the ball. I try to get on base any way possible. I am playing a cat-and-mouse game with the pitcher. The consistency of the umpire is also crucial to my success.

Tom Pagnozzi

Danny Tartabull

I try to hit a ground ball through the middle of the infield, in order to take advantage of my speed. I always look to make solid contact. A fine line exists between being passive and aggressive when selecting a pitch to hit. When there are men on base, I am aggressive. I do not go to bat thinking I will take a pitch. I hit if the ball is in my zone.

For me to be successful, I have to stay back and use my hands. I am a hand hitter, and I must give them a chance to get to the ball. I try to stay within myself when hitting.

I mentally think about what I want to do, and I focus in on the task at hand. I put on a game face of intensity, and yet I try not to lose my composure. In the on-deck circle, I try to size up the situation. I envision different situations and make the adjustments accordingly.

91

Jay Johnstone

If a pitcher strikes me out on a certain pitch, I try to remember it because I know I will see it again. Good work habits are important, and so is plenty of practice. It's important to work on going to the opposite field. When I played, I studied the pitchers, and I also had good knowledge of the catchers. I have always believed in good concentration.

I took it one game at a time. I did not worry about the pitcher too much because I could anticipate his pattern. The only way to hit a good change up is to be able to anticipate it.

Confidence is a special feeling that I carried throughout my career. Concentration allows you to see the ball well. To me, it was important to be a team player. I strived for consistency, and once I was in the ballpark, it was all work. Maybe two or three times a season you go into a slump, but with a level head and good work habits, they will not last long.

Johnny Ray

I am not a power hitter, so I have to make contact and hit at a high average to be effective. I believe in standing back and hitting the ball where it is pitched. I try to keep it simple and basic.

While I'm at bat, I try to keep my weight back and use as little movement as possible. I try to make contact, put the ball in play, make something happen.

It's important to be mentally prepared for the ups and downs, but especially for the downs. If you can do that, they will not last as long. There were times physically when I was not ready to play, so I would have to pick myself up mentally

Jay Johnstone

Johnny Ray

to succeed. Injuries, especially a wrist injury, can be devastating.

Vince Coleman

Good, consistent mechanics allow a player to get hits. Good mechanics help a hitter overcome prolonged slumps. Everything is timing, and when I'm in a groove, I see everything well and I'm hard to fool. The swing is effortless, the body is calm, and you have a good feeling of relaxation.

The swing should be loose and free. When I am in the on-deck circle, I observe what's happening on the field. I ask myself who is on base, who is behind me, is there a double-play situation? I am aware of the score.

I play the game one day at a time, one game at a time, and one at bat at a time. I don't set any goals, and I don't expect an end. I try to keep

from having mental fatigue. It is important not to think too much while at bat. Hitting is 90 to 95 percent mental, and too much thinking clouds the mind. The idea is to keep the thoughts clear and focused, and this requires concentration. I try to learn from my slumps and use them to my advantage.

Hal McRae

For me, the most important factor in hitting is the start because it is the first movement made. It's a negative movement, away from the pitcher.

While I am teaching, I try to stay as basic as possible. I work on stance, balance, start, locking of the head [down] at the point of contact, and hitting through the ball. These are the absolutes of hitting.

My mental criteria for hitting are confidence, concentration, and relaxation.

Vince Coleman

Hal McRae

George Scott

I always hit what I saw. I looked for a fastball and made adjustments to everything else. I was a situation hitter. If the situation called for a sacrifice fly, I tried to hit the bottom half of the ball. If it called for a base hit, I tried to hit the middle of the ball. Pitchers throw differently depending on the situation, and you have to adjust. I tried to keep a journal on all the pitchers' strategies against me.

Good hand and eye coordination are very important to hitting. When I was in the on-deck circle, I didn't worry about how the pitcher would throw to others, only how he would pitch to me. I would look for pitch location, the break of the ball, and whether the pitcher was wild high or low.

I always arrived at the ballpark early so I could take my time, observe, and prepare myself mentally for the game. Maintaining good concentration is the key to consistency and many productive years. When Hank Aaron came to Milwaukee, I asked him how he had so many consistent good years. He answered, "By maintaining concentration." You must always make adjustments to your game. A hitter can give up four or five at bats, but he cannot go thirty at bats before making the proper adjustment.

Hubie Brooks

I try to work with what the pitcher gives me. The most important thing for me is to keep my weight back. If I don't, the ball seems to get to the dish quicker.

George Scott

Hubie Brooks

I consider the confrontation between me and the pitcher to be a battle. I must bear down and concentrate. When I'm in a groove, I'm in total isolation. I hear nothing and see nothing but the ball.

Todd Zeile

I look middle away and adjust to the inside pitch. This makes me use the entire field, which is mandatory for major leaguers. To be successful, I feel I have to stay back, use my hands, and make adjustments around the plate.

Mentally I try to stay at a medium level, not get too high or too low. In order to be consistent through the years, a player must avoid injuries, have some luck, stay within himself, and just let things happen.

Glenn Braggs

If you can time the fastball, you can hit any other pitch. The fastball is usually the pitcher's best pitch. If you can take that away, he has to adjust. Once he does that, he's on the defensive.

When you're at bat, don't think about the mechanics much. Concentrate on getting the bat through the strike zone.

As a batter, I liked to crowd the plate, and look middle in. With two strikes I would cover the entire plate. I always tried to keep my head still and my eyes on the ball.

I like to see balance in a swing. If you have balance, you can execute the proper swing. I believe that slow hands come from a slow mind. If your mind can react quickly, the hands will react quickly. If you have balance and the ability

Todd Zeile

Glenn Braggs

to pick up the ball, everything else will fall into place.

Buzzy Keller

I believe a hitter must execute a shifting of weight, bat speed, and bat control at the correct moment to ensure a synchronized, successful swing. Visualize, remember, and practice the successful swing and block the failures out of your mind.

Hitting is reacting to visual stimuli, reacting to action. You go from soft core to hard, which means focusing and tracking the pitch. The movement is from negative to positive—away from the pitcher, then toward the pitcher.

Grooves are those few times in a season when in hitting there is no thinking, the visual system is effective, and the physical is all programmed. Timing is something the pitcher will let the hitter know. It is not what is done, but when, and the hitter must get to the point where he does not have to think about it. It must come naturally, and the movements must flow continuously. Hard work and practice allow this to happen.

Confidence is believing and staying within oneself. The two-strike approach is hitting the pitcher's pitch:

1. Choke up on the bat. For every one-half inch that is choked, there is 10 percent more control of the business end of the bat gained.
2. Whatever the distance the bat is choked is the distance to move closer to the plate.
3. Move up in the batter's box closer to the pitcher because 80 percent of all two-strike pitches are off-speed or breaking pitches.
4. Look for the pitch middle and away.
5. Think opposite field or up the middle. With two strikes, the hitter should enlarge his strike zone in, out, up, and down by the width of two baseballs.

If there is a cardinal sin in baseball, it is taking a called third strike. With two strikes, the hitter is more aggressive and has the tendency to swing at more pitches simply because the pitcher may throw a great pitch or the umpire may blow one.

I believe that an off year results from injuries, change in work habits, or a tendency of laziness after coming off a good year.

When instructing, always say "do this" or "try this," but never "don't do this" or "don't do that" because a coach should never teach negatively. The last thing you learn about performing a skill will be the first thing that drops from the mind when put under stress, tension, or fear.

Studies have found:

- The hitter only has hundredths of a second to read the velocity, rotation, location, and trajectory of the pitch . . . [and] to calculate whether or not to swing at a given pitch. . . . For the average hitter, the time to commit a swing is $20/100$ or $1/5$ of a second.
- An 86 MPH fastball takes $40/100$ of a second to reach the plate from the time it is released until it enters the contact zone.
- An 87 MPH fastball takes $39/100$ of a second to reach the plate.
- An 88 MPH fastball takes $38/100$ of a second to reach the plate.
- An 89 MPH fastball takes $37/100$ of a second to reach the plate.
- A 90 MPH fastball takes $36/100$ of a second to reach the plate.
- A 95 MPH fastball takes $31/100$ of a second to reach the plate.
- An 86 MPH fastball with four seams rotates fourteen times while in flight to the plate.

- *An 86 MPH fastball with two seams rotates eleven to twelve times while in flight.*
- *A curveball with four seams rotates twenty-three to twenty-four times while in flight.*

- *With a fastball with four seams, the hitter will see a red blur.*
- *With a fastball with two seams, the hitter will see two red stripes.*

CHAPTER 12

THE 20 COMMANDMENTS OF HITTING: RECAP

1. As you take your stance, bend both of your knees slightly and bend slightly at the waist.
2. Hit with a closed stance.
3. Keep your head motionless throughout the swing.
4. See the pitch five feet away and complete your swing.
5. Rotate your wrists slightly in a continuous clockwise motion to set the rhythm.
6. As the pitcher goes into his windup, turn your front shoulder inward toward the plate, which automatically will drive your hands and the bat backward, without moving your hands away from your body.
7. Take a short stride.
8. Stride softly.
9. Once you see a hittable pitch, in a controlled and coordinated manner take the weight off your back foot and shift it forward, driving toward the pitch with your body.
10. Begin to rotate your hips *before* moving your shoulders and hands.
11. To create rhythm and movement, your first forward movement will be dropping your hands toward your body in order to be in the optimal position to hit the ball.
12. Your bottom hand pulls everything into motion.
13. Your hands should always be above the bat head and the ball.
14. As your hands approach the hitting area, your hands and wrists must be held back.
15. Don't commit your hands too soon.
16. As you begin the swing, lower your

front shoulder slightly and swing across the ball.

17. Throw the bat head forward toward the ball. *Don't* swing the bat.

18. Upon contact, snap your wrists and extend both arms away from your body.

19. Hit the ball when your weight shifts back to your center of gravity.

20. The ideal location to make contact with the ball is somewhere in the zone between your center of gravity and the distance forward to your stride leg.

THE PHYSICS OF HITTING

Gravity

Hitting a baseball is one of the most difficult sports skills known to man. It requires incredible vision, strength, coordination, and the ability to bring all these components together at just the appropriate time in order to connect the bat to the ball. There is no sweeter sound or better feeling than placing the meat part of the bat on the center of the ball. The men who play the game of baseball at its highest level fail at this endeavor two out of three times on average, so how can we reasonably expect our players, whether they be children or adolescents, to accomplish this remarkable feat each time they step to home plate? An understanding of what we are asking of our players, or perhaps what we are asking of ourselves, will enable us to take a more practical approach to how hitting should be accomplished.

Since baseball is played (to my knowledge) only on the planet earth, each player must contend with gravity. Gravity is the force that is always acting on any object. It would certainly be much easier to hit a four-hundred-foot home run on the moon. Gravity forces us to make certain dispensations in order to hit or throw the ball as far as we possibly can. For instance, in order to hit the ball the furthest to overcome gravity, the angle of collision of the bat with the ball is forty-five degrees. In order to hit the ball with the greatest amount of precision, the angle of collision is sixty degrees. To pop up requires an angle of collision of ninety degrees. To strike out requires an angle of zero degrees, and there is no collision.

Gravity is only one of many important physics principles that must be considered. We often have a tendency to teach or coach as we were taught or coached. Application of these physics principles can sometimes be compromised knowingly, or more often, unknowingly. The player becomes the one who suffers the consequences of the coach's ignorance. The player's performance is compromised because the technique of hitting should be based on these physics principles. It is the purpose of this chapter to introduce the world of science to the world of hitting. It can be a harmonious coexistence with a little knowledge of fundamentals. The fundamentals of hitting are the physics principles in action.

Planes of Movement

Movement occurs through three planes. The horizontal (x) plane is when the bat moves parallel to the ground. The vertical (y) plane is where the bat is perpendicular to the ground. The front-to-back (z) plane is the most significant, as this is the movement of the bat from back to front. The z plane is the plane where the greatest amount of rotation occurs. This rotation generates torque which applies greatest force.

The bat moves through each of these planes. It moves forward, down, and throughout. The longer the bat moves in the horizontal plane, the greater the possibility it will intercept a projectile (ball) moving in the same plane. The swing is not level throughout as momentum and acceleration could not be gained starting the bat from behind the head. It does move on the horizontal plane as it approaches the ball. The first movement of the bat is forward, then down, and then through. The through portion of the swing is the point at which the bat is most likely to intercept the ball. The

levers are longest when the bat is in this position and can generate the greatest amount of force and momentum. The levers break quickly after contact in order to decelerate the levers to reduce the risk of tearing muscles.

Hitting Leverage

The human body is made up of a complex system of simple machines called levers. Each body segment such as the forearm, thigh, or finger is a lever which can move independently of the other levers or in conjunction with the other levers. The more levers that are involved in an action, the more complex this leverage system becomes. Hitting a baseball utilizes every lever of the body to accomplish the action.

Each lever is comprised of three parts. The fulcrum is the point at which the lever is stabilized in order to move at one end (pivot point). The bat is a lever and the fulcrum is the point on the bat at which the top hand is placed on the handle. The closer the fulcrum is placed to the end of the bat, the longer the lever. If a hitter uses a choke grip, the top hand is the fulcrum for the bat head and the bottom hand is the fulcrum for the butt end of the bat. The point from the fulcrum to the point of application of force (where the muscle that applies the force is inserted on the bone) is called the force or moment arm. The point for the moment arm to be calculated depends on which muscle or muscles are used to apply the force to move the lever. The lever arm is the point from which the force is applied (moment arm) to the end of the lever. It is the resistance that the force must overcome in order to accomplish movement (length of the bat from the hand to the end).

Hitting requires the use of every body segment which means the bat is only one of many levers that must be used. The longer the lever, the greater the force that must be applied to move the lever. The human body uses many muscles to move one lever. The reason for this is that the muscles are not attached from one bone (lever) to another at right angles. Therefore, it requires many muscles be coordinated to apply the force to move the bat (lever). Since no muscle is attached at a right angle to the bone, the bone actually rotates when the force is applied. This rotation is called torque. The more muscles involved to apply force, the greater the torque. When a coach says roll the hands to the ball, he is using the principle of torque. The human body is a system of levers that utilizes torque for every movement. Since the hitter wants to hit the ball as hard as possible, the principle of torque allows that to happen.

The length of the lever has a great deal to do with the amount of force that is required to move it. Basically, the longer the lever (bat), the greater the force that must be applied to overcome inertia in order to move it. The shorter the bat, the less force required to overcome inertia and move it. There is another consideration to be addressed—momentum. Momentum considers the mass (weight) of an object and the velocity with which that object moves. Since the bat moves from a pivot point (fulcrum) of the top hand, the movement of the end of the bat is an arc. The greater the distance from the top hand, the greater the arc. The longer the lever, the greater the length of the arc. Once inertia is overcome and movement occurs, the longer and heavier bat will continue in

motion longer and can apply greater force to the next lever. The shorter bat can overcome inertia faster because it requires less force, but cannot sustain momentum. The longer bat has greater mechanical advantage once inertia is overcome, but less capacity to move quickly. The shorter bat can move quickly, but has less mechanical advantage.

To be most mechanically efficient, momentum that is gained from each segment (upper arm, forearm, hand, finger, etc.) is transferred to subsequent segments (levers). When hitting, the momentum chain starts with the toes, moves to the foot, then to the shank, the thigh, the vertebrae, the upper arm, the forearm, the hand, and the fingers. Each segment gets faster as it uses the momentum from the previous segment and applies its own force. The combination of all these forces is the resultant force applied through the bat to the ball.

Newton's Laws of Physics

Newton's first law states that an object at rest tends to remain at rest. An object in motion tends to remain in motion at a constant speed and along a straight path. The tendency of objects to resist changes in motion is called inertia. The only way an object can change its motion is to be acted upon by force. The muscles must exert a force in order to overcome the inertia of the bat when it is taken from the bat rack.

Newton's second law states that when force is applied to an object, it will accelerate. This acceleration is directly proportional to the net force (summation) and is inversely proportional to the mass. Acceleration is always in the direction that the net force is applied. The heavier the object, the greater the force required to move it. The heavier the bat, the stronger the hitter must be to move it.

Newton's third law states that for every action there is an equal and opposite reaction. Forces come in pairs—one comes in action, the other in reaction. Neither force can exist without the other. When one object exerts a force on another, the second exerts an equal and opposite force on the first.

These three laws are accepted as the basis for movement on earth. Each is directly applicable to hitting a baseball. The player must move the bat to the ball by applying a force which overcomes inertia (first law). This accelerates the bat to the ball (second law). These forces come from muscles which work in pairs (third law) so that when one muscle group shortens, the opposing muscle group lengthens.

Mechanics of the Swing

The swing moves with acceleration first and leverage second. To achieve acceleration:

- The elbows are flexed.
- The hips are flexed.
- The wrists are flexed.
- The trunk is fixed.

All move to extension for mechanical efficiencies, or leverage.

The swing begins with weight on the rear (dominant) foot. The rear hip and knee rotate to bring the hands forward. Each swing is begun the same way, whether the hands are released to the ball or kept back to check the swing.

In order to generate centrifugal force, weight must be positioned over the foot, which is where the rotation forward occurs. The large muscle groups begin the movement to overcome inertia. The rear hip and knee begin this initial movement which starts the hands forward.

The hands exploding through the hitting zone is the result of proper summation of forces applied at the joints prior to the hand movements—like driving a five-speed car:

- First gear is slow, but overcomes inertia and gets things moving (hips).
- Second gear is faster and allows for momentum to continue the car in motion (knees).
- Third gear is faster and allows for an increase in momentum (torso).
- Fourth gear is still faster and more efficient (shoulders).
- Fifth gear is fastest and most efficient (wrists).

The further into the mechanics of the swing, the less energy is expended to complete the swing.

Lexicon

acceleration The rate at which velocity changes with regard to time. Acceleration is positive change (increase). Deceleration is a negative change (decrease).

axis of rotation The line around which rotation occurs. The axis can be in any plane or combinations of planes. Rolling the top hand to the ball changes the axis of rotation of the bat head to the ball.

conservation of energy Energy cannot be created or destroyed. It may be transformed from one form to another, but the total amount of energy does not change at any point.

energy   Property of a body or system that allows it to do work. The muscles of the body allow the body to move to hit the ball and, therefore, accomplish work.

force   To push or pull against an object. The muscles of the body apply force to the bat which applies force to the ball. It is the product of the mass and acceleration.

fulcrum   The point at which the lever (bat) is stabilized to move at an end. It is the pivot point. The top hand is the fulcrum to move the bat head to the ball. If a choke grip is used, the bottom hand is the fulcrum for movement of the butt of the bat.

inertia   The resistance an object offers to changes in its state of motion. To overcome inertia, force must be applied. To move the bat to the ball, the muscles must apply force to overcome inertia.

kinetic energy   Energy in motion. A thrown or batted ball has kinetic energy.

lever   A simple machine employed for mechanical efficiency. The bat is a lever. Each body segment is also a lever. To generate the greatest amount of force, the hitter should utilize the greatest number of levers.

lever arm   The distance from point of application of force to the end of the segment. The final lever arm used in hitting a baseball is the distance from the top hand to the end of the bat. The greater the length of the lever arm, the greater the rotation (torque) of the object. The greater the rotation, the greater the resultant force applied to the ball.

mass   The quantity of matter of an object. It is the measurement of the inertia (sluggishness) that an object offers in response to an effort to change its state of motion. The space and weight a bat occupies is considered its mass.

momentum   Mass of an object multiplied by its velocity.

plane   The line of movement an object takes. The three planes for movement to be analyzed are horizontal (x), vertical (y), and front to back (z). Combinations of any or all planes result in rotation. The bat head moves in all three planes to hit the ball.

potential energy   Energy that is stored. Stretched muscle groups (like stretched rubber bands) have potential energy until movement occurs, at which point it becomes kinetic. Contact with the ball is the result of both potential and kinetic energy.

power   The amount of work done per unit of time taken to accomplish it. If a person hits with power, he can accomplish the same amount of work within a shorter time period. Power equals work done divided by time interval.

projectile   An object that is in motion as a result of force and continues in motion by virtue of its own inertia. The ball is a projectile that can be thrown or batted.

resultant   The net result of combining two or more vectors. Resultant force applied to the ball is accomplished with force (muscles), velocity (speed and direction) of body segments, acceleration, and momentum of the bat. The combination of these is resultant force.

scalar   A quantity that has magnitude but not direction, such as mass and speed. Weight and space the bat and ball occupy are scalar quantities that are necessary to calculate acceleration and force.

speed   Distance traveled per time frame. Speed has no direction.

torque Changes the rotation of the bat. The greater the distance from the axis of rotation (the longer the bat), the greater the amount of torque. The longer the lever arm, the longer it takes to overcome inertia and move the bat to the ball.

vector Something that has both magnitude and direction such as force, velocity, acceleration, and momentum. Hitting a baseball uses all these vectors to accomplish the skill.

velocity Speed of an object with a specified direction. The pitcher throws a ball with speed (rate), but also in a direction (the plate). The hitter hits the ball with speed and direction.

work The product of force and distance. Work is accomplished each time a ball is hit as movement (distance the bat moves) is accomplished. Work is also accomplished each time we pick up an object, such as a bat or ball, which has weight.

ASSESSMENT OF HITTING TECHNIQUE THROUGH COMPUTERIZED MOTION ANALYSIS

Here is a computer analysis of my swing from a sports training biomechanics center I attended in Irvine, California. These clinics exist all across America. For about $85, you can have your swing evaluated. I have personally taken more than 600 athletes, both amateur and professional, to get their swings filmed and analyzed. The likelihood is that you can go to the physiology department of about any college and find someone who can do this for you.

This report contains the results of a detailed assessment of hitting technique performed through the utilization of high-speed video recording and subsequent computerized motion analysis. The parameters of motion used in this study are based on the four essential and invariant elements of hitting: dynamic balance, kinetic link, bat lag, and axis of rotation. The type of hit assessed is a long fly pitched at the center of the plate.

The general format used for each section

of this report first defines ideal performance for the hitting element being discussed and then presents the results of analysis in the form of a computer-generated graph of relevant motion parameters. Numerical labels quantify the proximity to the ideal or the amount of error present in the measured motion parameters for the subject.

The dynamic balance graph shows the motion of the feet, the top of the head, and the center of gravity in the direction of the pitcher (the x axis).

The kinetic link graph shows the angular motion of the shoulder and hip segments as viewed from the vertical (y axis) direction, as well as the back-side knee-joint angle.

The bat lag graph shows the bat velocity in the direction of the pitcher (x axis).

The axis of rotation graph shows the motion of the head and center of gravity in the vertical direction (y axis).

The results of analysis are next presented

in tabular form, with each critical factor listed as "yes" or "OK" if performed correctly, "no" or "off by" a particular amount if performed incorrectly. An overall biomechanical performance index is provided to assist in the selection of remedial action, if required. Finally, a verbal diagnosis of the potential problems caused by observed deficiencies in each of the hitting elements is provided along with a prescription for correcting these problems through training and application of proper hitting technique.

Dynamic Balance

IDEAL

The dynamic balance is the motion of the balance point of the body (center of gravity) through the swing. The center of gravity (C.G.) must be central to the base of support (equidistant between the feet) starting at the stance and continuing through the swing to the point of contact. During the preparation, rhythm must stabilize prior to the stride. After completion of the stride, forward motion of the center of gravity must stop prior to contact.

Launch Position and Horizontal (X Axis) Body-Joint Positions

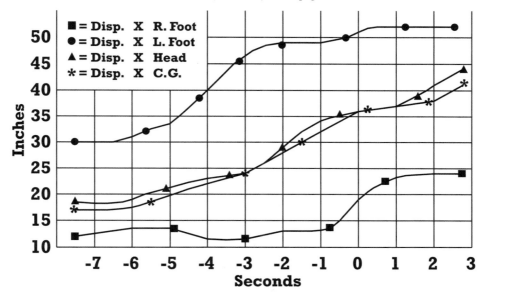

Dynamic Balance Assessment

Performance Index
88%
Effectiveness

Stabilization of Rhythm — Yes **X** No _____

		OK	off by
Stance length	18.6"	OK **X**	off by _____
C.G. at stance (<60% Stance)	5.9"	OK ___	off by _marginal_
Stride begins at	59 sec.	OK **X**	off by _____
Stride length (<60% Stance)	18.9"	OK **X**	off by _____
C.G. movement (<75% Stride) . . .	18.6"	OK ___	off by _4+"_
Head movement (<75% Stride) . .	16.8"	OK ___	off by _2+"_
Base at contact	37.3"	OK **X**	off by _____
C.G. at contact (50% Base)	24.1"	OK ___	off by _4+"_

Diagnosis: Stance is good but C.G. starts back and must move forward as much as you stride to catch up. This makes it difficult to achieve stability at contact and leaves your balance slightly forward of the center of your feet.

Prescription: Set up with your weight more balanced and with a slightly wider stance. Take a slightly shorter stride, ending up with the same base at contact. This will cut down on C.G. drift, improving stability and balance.

Kinetic Link

IDEAL

The ideal kinetic link produces high bat velocity by the sequential transfer of energy from the stronger and heavier body segments (legs and trunk) to the arms and finally to the bat. Energy generation begins at the feet, the base of support, with sequential transfer through the legs, hips, trunk, shoulders, arms, hands, and bat. Energy increases through the linked body segments, producing high bat velocity.

Contact Position and Body-Segment Angles

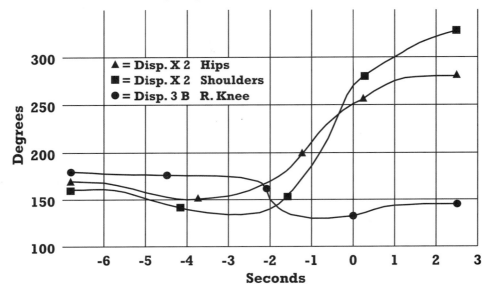

▲ = Disp. X 2 Hips
■ = Disp. X 2 Shoulders
● = Disp. 3 B R. Knee

Degrees (y-axis): 100, 150, 200, 250, 300
Seconds (x-axis): -6, -5, -4, -3, -2, -1, 0, 1, 2, 3

Kinetic Link Assessment

Stride Plant
Front-side foot at 45 degrees ......Yes **X** No___
Back-side heel up ....Yes **X** No___
Hips into rotation (open) ....Yes **X** No___
Shoulders Closed ....Yes **X** No___

Performance Index 89% Effectiveness

Approach to Contact
B foot (full rotation on toes) ....Yes **X** No___
B knee joint (<120 Degrees) ....Yes___ No **X**
Hips lead shoulders to Contact .....Yes___ No **X**

Diagnosis: Your hands and shoulders come around before your hips achieve full rotation. This reduces energy transfer and thus bat velocity at contact. Results from incomplete front-side blocking in the stride phase.

Prescription: Keep your hands and shoulders back until you have initiated full hip rotation. At contact your hips should be square to the pitcher for maximum power transfer into your upper body and arms. Hip rotation will also be reflected in back-knee angle.

	1	2	3	4	5	6	7	8	9	10	R	H	
VISITORS	1	0		1	0						2		BALLS 1
HOME	0	0			1	0					3		STRIKES 2

Bat Lag

IDEAL

The hands and bat, the last kinetic link, lag back as the rest of the body segments rotate. The hands and bat move slightly back to a position near the shoulder and close to the chest as the stride begins. As the front foot plants, the wrists are cocked at the launch position. During the approach to contact, after the body has rotated, the path of the bat is linear and horizontal. Just before contact the front arm decelerates (blocks), transferring energy into the bat, which generates high angular bat velocity (whipping action).

Lag Position and Bat Velocity

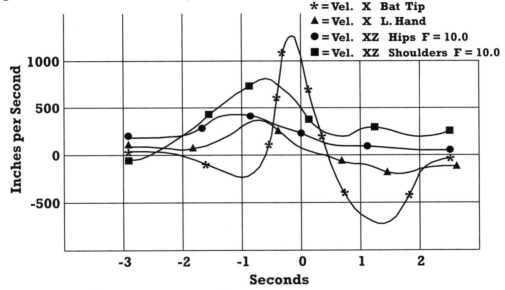

* = Vel. X Bat Tip
▲ = Vel. X L. Hand
● = Vel. XZ Hips F = 10.0
■ = Vel. XZ Shoulders F = 10.0

Bat Lag Assessment

Stance, Stride, and Launch
Bat and hands near shoulder . . . . .Yes **X** No __

Bat and hands close to chest . . . . .Yes **X** No __

Wrists cocked (bat angle) . . . . .Yes **X** No __

Approach and Contact
Takes knob to ball (bat horizontal) . . . . . .Yes **X** No _____

B arm in slot (upper arm angle) . . . . .Yes __ No marginal

Hips, shoulders lead hands, bat . . . . .Yes __ No **X** _____

Bat velocity (x .0568): 73.6 mph . . . . .OK **X** Slow _____

Performance Index 93% Effectiveness

Diagnosis: You achieve outstanding bat velocity with your present mechanics and could improve over this with more complete hip rotation while keeping your hands back a fraction of a second longer.

Prescription: Remember at stride plant to initiate a quick and powerful hip rotation, while trying to hold your hands, arms, and bat back as long as you can. This will actually give you a quicker bat once you launch by "loading" your trunk and arms. Otherwise very sound bat mechanics.

Axis of Rotation

IDEAL

The axis of rotation is the imaginary vertical line the body rotates around during the swing. This "vertical pole" should pass through the head and center of gravity (C.G.), intersecting the base of support equidistant between the feet. Rotation begins with the blocking of the front leg at the moment of foot plant and the simultaneous raising of the back heel. Forward movement of the head and center of gravity must end with front leg blocking. Emphasizing rotation in the swing maintains dynamic balance through contact and generates high bat velocity with more accuracy.

Post-Contact Position and Vertical (Y Axis) Movement

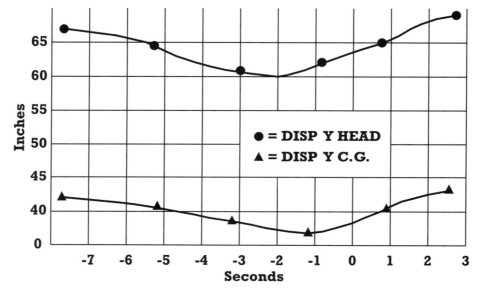

● = DISP Y HEAD
▲ = DISP Y C.G.

Axis of Rotation Assessment

Axis of Rotation
Center of gravity, head aligned . . . . Yes **X** No_____
Head central to base . . . . Yes___ No _marginal_
Center of gravity central to base . . . . Yes___ No **X**_____

Vertical Movement
Head level (<4″ movement) . . . . Yes___ No **X**
C.G. level (<3″ movement) . . . . Yes___ No **X**

Performance Index
84%
Effectiveness

Diagnosis: Though your head and center of gravity are aligned, your axis of rotation is inefficient due to dropping during your stride and drifting through contact. This reduces energy transfer from your lower body into trunk and arms.

Prescription: Work on stronger blocking with your front leg as your stride foot comes down. Strive for complete hip rotation to "load" your trunk from launch to contact. Start with a slightly wider base or bend knees more in your stance to prevent 6″ drop during your stride. This will improve consistency of contact.

APPENDIX C

SCOUTING HITTING ABILITY

Baseball is the hardest sport to scout. If you just look at the baseball draft, there have been several players drafted in the first round who never made it to the big leagues, or at least have not been stars in the big leagues: Al Chambers in Seattle, Bill Almon in San Diego, Brad Komiminsk in Atlanta, John Mizerock in Houston, Cecil Espy in Chicago, Robbie Wine in Houston, and several others we could name. It is almost impossible to scout a player's heart and desire to improve as a baseball player. If a player does not have that inner desire to be the best he can possibly be, he will not go too far.

The most important element in scouting hitting ability is bat speed—how fast a player can get the bat through the strike zone. Some teams just look for good athletes— players that can really run and throw. They believe if they can find these guys, they can teach them to hit. This is not true in all cases. You have to have some aptitude for hitting. You must have natural bat speed.

Quickness with the hands and wrists is an important phase of hitting. The ability to be quick with the hands, wrists, and arms will determine just how good a hitter the player is going to be. If a hitter can learn how to be fast with his hands and wrists, he will be able to wait longer for the pitch.

The only way to become a good hitter is to swing the bat constantly, not just when taking the few swings in batting practice. It is the desire to hit and the willingness to practice that makes the great hitters. While not every player can become a great hitter, every player can improve through instruction and practice.

Perhaps the two most important rules in hitting are keeping the bat level and having good timing. Successful hitting involves hitting outside pitches to the opposite field. Inside pitches, of course, should be pulled. Only constant practice at the plate, swinging at every type of pitch will give a hitter timing.

Perhaps the most discussed topic on hitting is the proper hitting swing. For years the majority of baseball authorities stressed the importance of the level swing; this is still dominant among batting instructors today.

The correct stance in hitting is whatever stance the player is most comfortable in. If you watch a baseball game on TV, you will see several different styles. A player must find a stance that is most comfortable to him.

Knowing the strike zone is also a very important aspect of hitting. Ted Williams once said, "The more critical you are in learning the strike zone, the easier it will be for you to develop into a good hitter. This is because you will be ahead of the pitcher. You will have him in the hole rather than yourself."

INDEX

Page numbers in **boldface** refer to illustrations.

types of focus in, 25
visualization and, 54–55, 96
willpower and, 54
Hitting zone, 46–47
Horizontal movement, 37
Hornsby, Rogers, 76
Hriniak, Walt, 40, 43

I

Incaviglia, Pete, 43
Inertia, 105
Injuries, 89

J

Jackson, Bo, 33
Johnstone, Jay, 92

K

Keller, Buzzy, 96
Kinetic energy, 105
Kinetic link, 107, 110

L

Lau, Charlie, 40
Leg movement, 36–44

Lever, 105
Lever arm, 105
Leverage, hitting, 102–4
Line drive base hits, 86
Line drive swing, 84
Luck, 76

M

McGee, Willie, 54, 57, 70, 89
McRae, Hal, 73, 93
Mass, 105
Mattingly, Don, 26, 71
Mental confidence, 88
Mental preparation, 85, 86, 87, 88, 89, 91, 92, 95
Mental rehearsal, 77
Mind, the, 78
Mind control, xiii
Mitchell, Kevin, 86
Modified choke grip, 8, **9**
Momentum, 105
Morgan, Joe, 17
Movement, planes of, 102

O

Obsessions, 77–78
Oliva, Tony, 73–74
Open stance, 15, **16**, 86
Oquendo, José, 15
Overlapping finger grip, 8, **9**, **11**
Overmire, Stubby, 54, 79

P

Pagnozzi, Tom, 24, 91
Palmeiro, Rafael, 43
Patience, 57, 83, 88, xiii
Physics, Newton's laws of,
      103–4
Pitchers, 76, 83, 90
Pitching, xiv
Plate
      coverage, **18**, 18–19
      foot placement on, 16–17
      positioning at, 17–18
Positive thought, 77
Potential energy, 105
Power, 105
Power hitters, 9
Practice, batting, 69–72, 84
      mental preparedness and,
            72–74
Projectile, 105
Pull hitters, 80

Q

Quickness, 113

R

Raines, Tim, 63, 71, 73, 88
Ray, Johnny, 51–52, 73, 92–93
Relaxation, 56–57, 77
Responsibility, 58
Resultant, 105

Rhythm, 30–32, 88
Roberts, Bip, 55
Rocking, during swing, 37
Rose, Pete, 52, 55, 56
Ruth, Babe, 44

S

Sandberg, Ryne, 69–70, 71, 72–73,
      86–87
Scalar, 105
Scott, George, 73, 94
Scouting, for baseball, 113–14
Shifts, 79
Sierra, Ruben, 33
Skill memory, xiii
Slumps, hitting, 63–66
Smith, Dwight, 73
Smith, Ozzie, 30, 31, 44, 84–85
Soft-center focus, 25
Speed, 105
Spray hitters, 9–10, 17
Square stance, **17**
Stance, 13–14, 86, 87
      crouching in, 14–15
      head placement and, 19–20
      open, 86
      proper, **14**
      types of, 15–16, **16**, **17**, **18**
      weight distribution and, 20
Straightaway stance, 15
Streaks, hitting, 66–67
Stride, 32–34, 86–87
Strike zone, 75–76, 114
Swing, the, 35
      body coordination and, 36–44
      hitting zone and, 46–47